TEACHING TEACHERS TO TEACH

A Basic Manual for Church Teachers

Donald L. Griggs

A Griggs Educational Resource

published by
Abingdon Press / Nashville

This manual is dedicated to all of the teachers who have helped me shape my thinking about teaching and learning. The teachers who have influenced me most are those who have attended the hundreds of workshops I have conducted throughout the United States. These teachers have shared experiences, asked questions, challenged statements and demonstrated expertise that have proven in many ways that teachers have a lot to learn from each other.

Teaching Teachers to Teach

TEACHING TEACHERS TO TEACH

A BASIC MANUAL FOR CHURCH TEACHERS

TABLE OF CONTENTS

Introduction		1
Chapter One	Roles of the Teacher	2
Chapter Two	Ten Curriculum Decisions Teachers Must Make	4
Chapter Three	Focus on Key Concepts	6
Chapter Four	Focus on Instructional Objectives	12
Chapter Five	Focus on Teaching-Learning Activities	17
Chapter Six	Focus on Teaching-Learning Resources	24
Chapter Seven	Practice the Planning Process	36
Chapter Eight	Criteria for Evaluating Lesson Plans	44
Chapter Nine	The Art of Asking Questions	47
Chapter Ten	Creative Use of Media	54
Chapter Eleven	Values and Teaching in Church Education	67
Chapter Twelve	Ways to Increase Student Participation	80
Chapter Thirteen	Designing Teacher Education Events	89
	a. Importance of Teacher Education	89
	b. Some Thoughts About Recruiting and Support of Teachers	89
	c. Types of Teacher Education Events	94
	d. Teacher Education for Churches Without Professional Staff	96
	e. Necessary Components to all Teacher Education Events	97
	f. Ten Descriptions of Teacher Education Events	98
Bibliography		109

INTRODUCTION

Teaching is not as much a science as it is an art. The teacher is more an artist than he is a scientist. There are too many variables, too many unpredictable factors in even one hour of classroom activities which prevent us from becoming scientific about teaching and learning. If teaching were a science, then all we would have to do is master the proper formulae for a given situation and we would be guaranteed success. But, teaching is not a science; there is no one right way to teach a given class or particular subject or to approach a group of students. Teaching is an art that must be developed, practiced, and evaluated for its effectiveness.

Even though teaching is not a science there are many specific steps and techniques which teachers can employ that will lead to more effective teaching. Art has its structure and style. There is a discipline that every artist accepts. There are rules to follow and criteria to consider. That is true of teaching, also.

This manual is an attempt to identify and systematize some of the basic elements of teaching and learning in the church. We cannot cover everything but we can uncover some of the essential ingredients to effective teaching.

There are two groups of persons for whom this manual is designed — the regular, volunteer, non-professional **classroom teachers** and the salaried, employed, professional **church educators. Classroom teachers** are those who relate to students on a regular basis and are responsible for planning teaching-learning activities for an hour or more each week. **Church educators** are persons who are employed by churches on a full-time or part-time basis, to be responsible for the overall direction and support of teachers and teaching in the church.

Classroom teachers will find the first twelve chapters especially helpful to them. The focus in the first two chapters is on the role of the teacher and some decisions teachers must make week by week. The next six chapters focus on the planning process and the essential components to every lesson plan. If two or more teachers work together in reading these six chapters it will be possible to actually participate in a team planning process. There are suggested exercises or activities for each person to do to practice the planning process. In chapters nine through twelve, four general topics are presented which offer suggestions to teachers of ways to implement specific techniques and resources in their teaching.

Chapter thirteen has six sections which are designed particularly for **church educators** who are concerned about providing support and training for the teachers for whom they are responsible. The last section offers ten designs for teacher education events based upon the content presented in the first twelve chapters.

For those readers who have read other books that I have written — most particularly THE PLANNING GAME — or have attended workshops I have conducted, there will be much in this manual that is familiar. However, in this manual I have, for myself and others, gathered a lot of my ideas and teaching strategies in one place.

This manual will be most helpful if the reader works one chapter at a time, beginning with the first. The church educator could start with chapter thirteen but that chapter will make more sense after considering the content of the first twelve chapters.

CHAPTER ONE

ROLES OF THE TEACHER

Teachers perform many roles in the classroom. After a busy session with paint, poster, or collage materials the teacher may feel that the role of **janitor** is most fitting. Or, when a student is troubled and needs someone to talk to the role of **counselor** may be most appropriate. We could probably list a dozen or more roles teachers act out in the course of several sessions of teaching. In this chapter we want to focus on four especially important roles.

Perhaps the most important role a teacher can play is that of being a **friend** to the students. We are not talking about a buddy-buddy relationship. We are emphasizing the personal, caring, loving, being-with relationship that is important for persons to be able to communicate and grow with each other. Reflect for a moment on the teachers you have had as a student in the church or school. Try to bring into focus one or two particular teachers whom you would identify as having been friends to you. What do you recall about them as persons or the way they acted that makes you think of them as friends? I have asked this question of many persons and I have heard many responses which included statements such as . . .

"We had opportunities to know them outside the class."
"Mrs. _____ always called us by name."
"Sometimes Mr. _____ would visit with us and our parents at home."
"They really listened and cared about what we had to say."
"They were interesed in things we were interested in."

And, I am sure you could add to the list with your own observations of what it is that makes you remember certain teachers as friends. Most students who complete four years of high school and college will experience more than two hundred teachers. What a tragedy it would be if some of those teachers were not remembered as friends.

The important point is that we have a chance to be remembered by the students we teach as persons who are their friends. The students will remember us as persons long after they have forgotten the specific subjects we have taught.

Even though this whole manual is focused upon skills, techniques, activities and resources that contribute to effective teaching we must keep at the center of our attention the realization that the relationships we establish in our classrooms are of primary importance. God has always worked and spoken through persons. **We are the persons** in the classrooms where we teach through whom God will speak to boys and girls, men and women.

Another role that is important is the role of teacher as **translator**. Teachers serve much better in the role of translators than they do as transmitters. A transmitter sends messages in one direction, from the source to the receiver. The problem with this mode of communication is that the success of the communication rests in the hands of the receiver. The receiver can decide whether to tune in or not, whether to switch channels or whether to turn the volume up or down. My observations in many classrooms have confirmed that what are sometimes identified as discipline problems are not but rather are examples of students changing channels or tuning out transmitter teachers.

The teacher will be much more effective as a **translator**. A translator is someone who helps facilitate communication between persons who are otherwise unable to communicate with each other. The translator has to listen very carefully. The translator must be familiar with the languages, frames of reference, and background of both parties. That is what is needed in the church too; teachers who listen, teachers who are familiar with both the world of the church and the world of the student. If teachers serve more as translators they will find that students become much more involved and motivated to learn.

There is an important role of the teacher that no teacher volunteers for. Most teachers assume that this role is fulfilled by someone else. We are referring to the role of teacher as **curriculum writer.** To recruit teachers with the understanding that they are to serve as curriculum writers will probably make the job much more difficult because very few teachers feel qualified to be curriculum writers. However, before we dismiss that role let's look at it in another way.

The curriculum that is produced by denominational or independent publishing houses is what teachers receive to use in their teaching. Usually the curriculum consists of a teacher's manual, student's book, and resource packets for each grade level. Whether the curriculum is excellent or poor is not the primary concern at this point. The fact is the curriculum is very general. It is written for a national market of teachers and students in general. The curriculum is only half written for a particular class. Only the teacher can adapt, tailor, and fit the curriculum for a group of students with specific skills, interests, abilities and previous experiences. Only the teacher in the classroom can determine whether or not a particular activity is appropriate for all, some or none of his class.

If we said that one of the roles of the teacher is **lesson planner** that would be no surprise or shock. Well, the lesson that is planned and used with a group of students is the curriculum they experience. Therefore, teachers must be helped to think and make decisions in the way that curriculum writers do. We are not suggesting that the teachers dispense with the curriculum provided by the church and start from scratch to write their own. We are suggesting that teachers assume some responsibility for tailoring the curriculum so that it fits the specific class.

The next chapter focuses on ten curriculum decisions that teachers must make. This whole manual is intended to help teachers to become more skillful as curriculum writers.

The fourth role of the teacher that is very important is that teachers continue to be **learners.** I think that the best adult education program a church can have is a motivated, responsible staff of teachers. Teachers should expect to learn a lot about children, about teaching, and about the biblical and theological concepts they are teaching.

When teachers serve as friends, translators, curriculum writers and learners then we can almost guarantee that teaching and learning will be exciting and rewarding for both teachers and students.

CHAPTER TWO
TEN CURRICULUM DECISIONS TEACHERS MUST MAKE

In the process of planning for teaching and implementing that plan, teachers must make many, many decisions. Even without a plan in an informal setting teachers must decide . . .

- who will I call on next?

- what questions will I ask?

- how can I get Andy more involved?

- what will I say in response to that question?

Consciously or unconsciously, teachers are called upon to make many decisions in the course of an hour's session. A problem many of us face as teachers is that we do not deliberately consider several alternative actions or responses, then choose the one that is most appropriate. Many times we react too quickly and do the first thing that comes to mind. With a little more careful planning and an awareness of some of the more important decisions that must be made, all teachers can become more effective in their teaching.

The ten decisions that are included in the following outline are not the only decisions a teacher must make. However, these are some of the very important decisions. Keeping the checklist of questions in mind when planning and teaching may help the teacher direct his teaching more purposefully. Each of the ten decisions, or areas of concern, is explored more thoroughly in other chapters in this manual. Also, there are many excellent books which can help a teacher explore more thoroughly each of the subjects. Some of the books that I like are included in the Bibliography at the end of the manual.

1. **What will I teach?**

   — The curriculum is a starting place, but there is too much.

   — I must select the key concepts to focus my teaching.

   — Concepts are words that persons use to represent experience, thoughts, objects, etc., to communicate with others.

   — Concepts are the focus of all teaching.

   — It is important to relate concepts to the life-experience of the students.

2. **What will the students learn?**

   — It is important for teachers to have specific objectives in mind toward which they direct their planning and teaching.

   — Objectives express what teachers intend for the students to achieve in a period of instruction.

   — Objectives should be specific in terms of student action.

   — Objectives help the teacher to evaluate what happened.

3. **What teaching activities will I plan for the session?**

   — A variety of teaching activities will involve most of the students most of the time.

   — Teaching activities should represent different levels of interest and ability.

   — New activities should be introduced and tried out regularly.

4. **What resources will the students and I use?**

   — Resources are not just gimmicks and gadgets.
   — Resources are those means by which students get involved to participate in their own learning.
   — Resources must be selected carefully.
   — Resources are for students and teachers.
   — A wide variety of resources should be used.

5. **What strategy will I use to motivate students to be involved?**

   — It takes a carefully worked out strategy to engage the students with interest and purpose in their study.
   — There are at least five elements to the strategy which include Opening, Presentation, Exploration, Creativity and Closing.

6. **How will the room be arranged?**

   — The room arrangement, decoration, and display of resources teach as much as the words we use.
   — Allow for maximum visibility of all materials and easy movement of all students.
   — Rearrange the furniture, equipment, displays, and materials regularly.

7. **What questions will I ask?**

   — Questions are an important, necessary activity.
   — It will help to plan key questions ahead of time.
   — There are at least three levels of questions to use which include Information, Analytical and Personal questions.

8. **What choices will the students make during the session?**

   — Student choices lead to greater motivation and involvement.
   — Choices should be considered for every step of the lesson plan.
   — Choices need to be discussed and evaluated.

9. **What directions will I give?** ·

   — The success of students in the learning activities is often determined by the kinds of directions the teacher gives.
   — Students are guided in their participation by the teacher's directions.
   — Directions should be visible as well as verbal.
   — Directions should be given in several steps.

10. **How will I respond after a student says or does something?**

   — A teacher's reinforcement of students leads to great participation by the students.
   — Students need to receive feedback or responses from their teachers.
   — Teachers can develop a repertory of responses.

The rest of this manual is intended to help teachers explore further the subject of each of these decisions or questions.

CHAPTER THREE
FOCUS ON KEY CONCEPTS

To focus on key concepts is to respond to the question raised in the first of the teacher's decisions listed above, "What will I teach?"

Before planning a lesson or entering the classroom the teacher must consider the subject matter to be taught. The teacher usually has help making this decision because the curriculum that is provided has an outline of the scope and sequence of the subject matter for the whole year. There are other sources of direction to guide the teacher in deciding what to teach. The season of the year; the current events of the world, nation, or community; the suggestions of pastors, directors and superintendents; as well as the needs and interests of the students all influence to some degree what will be taught.

Most teachers have commented, "There is too much to teach. I will never be able to cover it all if I had twice as much time." That is true! There is too much to teach. For some reason teachers labor under the illusion that they must "cover" it all, if not in one lesson, then certainly during the year they should "cover" everything. That is impossible! Teachers cannot even teach everything that is provided for them in the curriculum materials. Editors and authors of curriculum prepare their materials for a national market. They write for a wide variety of teaching situations and must provide more than could be used by any one teacher.

Teachers must participate actively and responsibly in the process of deciding what to teach. Teachers need to be selective. Since they cannot teach everything, then teachers should select key concepts which will provide a focus for one or more sessions. If teachers are tempted to feel responsible for "covering" all the material, they should be reminded that there is another way to look at "to cover . . ." **"To cover is to hide something from view."**

When teachers overload students with a lot of concepts that is exactly what happens — much is hidden from view. The task of the teacher instead is to "uncover . . .", "to uncover" key concepts so that they can be presented, comprehended, and used with clarity and meaning.

When being selective of key concepts to teach, teachers must be concerned about several factors.

Concepts are basic to our teaching in the church. The dictionary defines "concept" as a "thought or an opinion: a mental image of a thing formed by generalization from particulars." Something that is omitted from this definition is that concepts are mostly derived from one's experience. A person's experiences of "love," "church," "father" will influence to a large degree his concepts of them. In teaching in the church we confront students who bring with them a wide variety of experiences with already-formed concepts so that the process of communication and teaching is not an easy one.

Consider, for example, the concept of "shepherd" in "the Lord is my shepherd." For a nomadic Hebrew who lived with sheep, who was either himself a shepherd or whose family included some shepherds, it was not difficult to think of God as being like a shepherd.

God guides, cares for, and protects persons the way a shepherd provides for his sheep. What about a child in an urban or suburban community who has never seen, touched, heard, or smelled a sheep? Or has never seen a shepherd? How can he form an appropriate concept of shepherd as intended in Psalm 23? The only concept of shepherd one girl had was that her pet dog was a German shepherd. She was really confused when she was first introduced to "the Lord is my shepherd."

What this suggests to me is that concepts taught in the church school will be more easily grasped if they can somehow be related to the experience level of the students. Shepherd to a Hebrew in Israel was a very concrete, real concept, but to an urban student it is a very abstract concept. The more abstract a concept is, the more open it is to misunderstanding and the more difficult it is to teach.

a. **Start where the learner is.** As teachers we have become very familiar with concepts like "God is love," "The Bible is the word of God," and many more. However, for students there is not the same familiarity. Students in our classes will hear for the first time concepts that are very familiar to us. But we must start where the learner is, building concepts on experiences that are appropriate to the learner.

b. **Begin with concepts based upon the learner's experience.** If students come to the classroom with limited experience of the Moses stories, then we can be the means of providing the experience. Before talking about the Hebrews as slaves we need to be sure the students can identify what a slave is.

c. **Reinforce what is taught by comparison and repetition.** The parables of Jesus are good examples of this process. Students learn quickly and what they learn is retained when they are actively involved in the process of comparing factors related to the particular concepts. Repetition need not be boring recitation, but rather a reworking of the same material in a different way.

d. **Be selective; focus on one concept at a time.** We tend to try to teach too much. When we introduce a hundred concepts in an hour, we are sure to confuse the student. We need to be selective by teaching a few key concepts well and not worrying about all those other concepts that were not included in this session. Better to teach a few concepts well than to cover dozens of concepts lightly.

Related to this subject on key concepts in teaching are some excerpts from an article by Dr. Edgar Dale, a Professor of Education at Ohio State University, in *The News Letter*, March 1970.

EDUCATION AS CONCEPTUALIZING

"Education is a process of developing and refining concepts, applying them to old and new situations. A concept is a generalized idea about a class of objects or events. It deals with our experiences — tangible or intangible, concrete or abstract. To master a field of subject matter is to learn its key concepts. These concepts include not only its technical terms but also its principles or generalizations. A concept may be a word, a principle, or a combination of the two. A concept may be limited or it may be an overarching concept, a basic design for learning.

"Some concepts are readily mastered — the 3,000 or so words that children bring with them to the first grade. Others are developed with ingredients that only age or mature reflection can provide, e.g., justice, love, responsibility. In all concept development there is a process of distillation, moving from imprecision to precision. The concepts may be denotative, with high fences around them, or connotative, rich with reminding.

"I believe that we would have a revolution in education if all teachers understood the most effective way to develop concepts, realized the necessary stages through which most concepts develop. I see three major categories which can be identified on the sacle from concrete to abstract.

"First, we have the overt, concrete event itself in all its rich sensory appeal. It may be seen, handled, heard, tasted, smelled. It contains the rich juices of life, not yet dried up. It is first-handed experience, not second, or third-hand.

"Second, as we move along the concrete-abstract scale, many experiences are representations of first-hand experiences — condensed somewhat, rearranged, but still recognizable as directly related to the original thing or event. A photograph or a moving picture, a model, a simulation, a dramatization, a painting is a semi-concrete experience.

"Finally, on the scale from concrete to abstract we come to experiences so fully condensed, so changed, that they no longer resemble the concrete or semi-concrete experience in any way. They have been "de-sensed." We have moved then from the event to the sign, and finally to the symbol. Jerome Bruner has called these three levels; doing, picturing, and symbolic. In discussing instructional media I have often used the model of a "Cone of Experience" to show the change from firsthand, direct, purposeful experience at the bottom of the cone to the highly condensed, abstract experience at the apex of the cone.

"Why is this discussion of concept building so important to the teacher? The great hazard of all teaching is a premature emphasis on the abstraction before the learner is "concretely" ready for it. Walt Whitman has good advice for us here: "(Language is) not an abstraction of the learn'd or of dictionary-makers, but it is something arising out of the works, deeds, ties, joys, affections, tastes of long generations of humanity, and has its bases broad and low, close to the ground."

"In thinking about the mastery of concepts we must not forget the most important concept of all, our self-concept. Is the image in our personal mirror one of pride or of rejection? Have most people learned to test their full powers, learned to work to the limits of their capacity? Since most people do not use more than fifty to sixty per cent of their potential, they should be able to increase sharply the quality and quantity of their concepts, read markedly better, use their time less wastefully, improve the quality of their human relations."

AN ACTIVITY TO PRACTICE FOCUSING ON KEY CONCEPTS

Take time to participate in the following activity which helps to reinforce some of the things we have considered in focusing on key concepts.

STEP ONE — Make a list of Key Words

In the blank space below or on a piece of scratch paper write down five or six key words that you would use to express something important about JESUS.

JESUS

1.   4.

2.   5.

3.   6.

STEP TWO — Compare your lists of Words

If you are doing this with another person, or several others, **compare your lists** of five or six words with each other. If you are doing this activity by yourself then **compare your list** of five or six words with my words. As you compare your lists, look to see how many of your words are similar to or different from the other's.

My list of words focusing on JESUS.

1. teacher   3. is alive today

2. God's representative   4. suffering servant

3. Messiah   5. truly man

STEP THREE — Consider Two Factors

As a result of what we have just done there are two factors worth considering:

1. No two persons choose exactly the same five or six key concepts to focus on Jesus. The more persons participating in the activity the more total number of words there will be.

   If we really do have different concepts that are important to each of us then how can we ever assume that our particular way of thinking or expressing ourselves about Jesus is the only way or the right way.

   This is a good demonstration of why the teacher must act as a **translator** (listening to and accepting the student's way of thinking) rather than as a transmitter (assuming that what teacher has to say is the only way or the best way).

2. Even though no two lists are identical there probably are one or two words that are similar when comparing two or three lists.

This suggests that even though we think and express ourselves in unique ways there is much that we have in common on a given subject. We do have concepts that we share and this is a good place to begin in our study and work together.

This is another good example of why it is important to be a translator — to start where the other person is, to begin with what we have in common and to build upon that.

STEP FOUR — Make a Composite List

On a chalk board or piece of newsprint or in this manual, make a composite list of all the words from the several lists. If it is just you and me, then combine our two lists to use for the next step.

List all the words:

— teacher   — alive today
—   —
—   — suffering servant
— God's representative   —
—   —
— Messiah   — truly man

STEP FIVE — Put All the Concepts in Two Categories

Look at all the words and place each in one of two categories: **concrete** or **abstract.** Concrete concepts are related to direct experiences; you can close your eyes and have a mental image of a concrete concept. You can draw a picture of a concrete concept. Abstract concepts are more symbolic; it takes more abstract concepts to explain or describe an abstract concept.

When you put the list of words in these two categories what do you notice? Are most of the words in the **abstract** category? This is not surprising because we are adults and as adults we have become able to think abstractly and to use abstract concepts with meaning.

But, that is not true of younger students or those unfamiliar with these concepts. Persons begin to make sense of concepts when they can connect the concepts to something concrete, to something in their own experience.

STEP SIX — Relate Concepts that Belong Together

Look at the list of words again. Select three or more words from the list that have something in common with each other. Then give that list of words a title. The title for the words indicates their commonality — they belong together in one category. For example, if we had the words: "teaches, preaches, leads, and prays" in one list we could give them the title **Actions of Jesus** or **Works of Jesus.**

Work on your own category of words and title.

Title: _____

1.   4.

2.   5.

3.   6.

You can add some other words to your category that were not in the original list.

There is an example of one way you decide what to teach; select concepts and focus on those that belong together. It is more helpful to students to work with concepts that have a connection with each other than to work with random sets of concepts.

STEP SEVEN — Summarize the Category with a Statement

Now that you have a set of words that belong together in one category, consider that you have a group of students to whom you want to communicate these concepts. Write two or three sentences keeping them as simple, concrete, and as connected to the central category as possible. The statement should be an expression of what you believe is important, that summarizes the essence of what you want to communicate.

Write your own statement . . . . .

These seven steps represent a process that helps a teacher respond to the question, "What will I teach?" Also, these steps suggest that it is important for teachers to respond to the question as **translators** and not as transmitters.

There will be another opportunity to put into practice what we have learned about key concepts when we get to chapter seven, **Practice the Planning Process.**

CHAPTER FOUR

FOCUS ON INSTRUCTIONAL OBJECTIVES

Whenever we plan a trip, a special meal, or a project around the house we usually have some specific objectives in mind; to arrive at Lake Tahoe on June 15, to have ten guests for dinner to be served at 7 p.m., or to finish painting the outside of the house during the two week's vacation. It is very easy to evaluate whether or not we achieved these objectives. Obviously, the objectives are not achieved just because we have stated them. It takes a lot of planning in order to achieve our intended objectives.

Objectives in teaching are somewhat similar. What we want to achieve with the students should be as specific as possible. We should be able to determine at the end of a session or unit of instruction whether or not the objectives for the students have been achieved.

A. First, some words of **definition:**

    1. **Objective** — noun
       "An aim or end of action; point to be hit; reached, etc."
       (Webster's New Collegiate Dictionary)

    2. **Objective —**
       "A collection of words describing a teacher's intent for the student."
       (Robert F. Mager)

    3. **"Behavioral objectives** are statements which describe what students will be able to do after completing a prescribed unit of instruction."
       (Kibler, Barker, and Miles)

B. **COMPARE GOALS WITH OBJECTIVES**

All church school curriculum is written with goals stated someplace in the introduction or other appropriate place. As teachers we usually have some goals in mind that we can state if someone asks us. Many times teachers use goals and objectives as synonymous. I think it is very important to distinguish the differences between goals and objectives. On the next page you will see a chart which is an attempt to summarize those differences.

C. Next, the **criteria for writing** instructional objectives:

    1. An objective should be written in terms of **student** performance. Does it say what we expect of the student?

    2. An objective should state in **observable** terms what students will be expected **to do.** Does it describe something we can **see** or **hear** the students do?

    3. An objective should be **specific.** Does it describe clearly and specifically what is expected of the student?

    4. An objective should state something of the **conditions** within which the student will be expected to perform. Does it indicate the condition that will influence a student's action?

(continued on page 14)

COMPARING GOALS AND OBJECTIVES

GOALS . . . are big enough to spend a whole lifetime pursuing.

. . . are beyond our reach; we will never fully achieve the goals of Christian living.

. . . give us direction for our teaching, learning, relating, deciding, etc.

. . . are too general to use for planning and evaluating teaching activities.

A person's growing toward a goal is influenced by many factors beyond the sphere of influence of the teacher.

A GOAL

"Persons will become more loving and caring toward other persons."

(sample)

The CLASSROOM

Learning activities and resources.

objectives

OBJECTIVES . . . are specific

. . . are written in terms of what students can be expected to accomplish, in particular learning activities.

. . . are achievable.

. . . are just little steps along the way toward the larger goal.

. . . are very helpful guidelines for teachers to use in planning and evaluating teaching activities.

. . . A person's achievement of objectives is directly influenced by the work of the teacher.

Objectives
"At the end of the period of study, the students will be able to visit an elderly person of the church to share a gift and conversation with that person."

(sample)

5. An objective should be **measurable.** Does it include a statement of quality of level of intended performance?

6. An objective should be **sequential** in relation to previous and following objectives. Does it relate in sequence to what preceded and what is to follow?

D. Start writing an objective with the following statement.

"At the end of the session(s) the students should be able to:"

> Comment: *This is a very helpful way to begin every instructional objective. It focuses on the **student** and what the teacher intends for him to be able to **do.***

E. After the introductory statement the next word is the key to the whole objective.

At the end of the session(s) the students should be able to:

understand . . . .
know . . . .
believe . . . .
realize . . . .   Avoid using words that are as general and
appreciate . . . .   non-specific as these are.
feel . . . .
acknowledge . . : . . . .

> Comment: *These words are too general. These are goal-oriented words. They do not help teachers determine whether students have accomplished what was intended. There is nothing wrong with "understanding," etc., per se, but as guidelines in planning for and evaluating teaching they are not very helpful.*

F. At the end of the session(s) the students should be able to:

demonstrate . . .	list	cite . . . .
compare	describe	follow . . . . . .
identify	show	quote . . . . . .
state	organize	name . . . .
create	write	summarize . . . .
explain	express	contribute . . . .
present	suggest	participate . . . .
apply	locate	select . . . . . .
find	discuss	ask . . . .

> Comment: *All of the above words are actions students can do which can be **seen** or **heard** by teachers. Such actions by students provide clues to the teacher that enable the teacher to evaluate more objectively whether or not students have achieved what teachers intended.*

AN ACTIVITY TO PRACTICE WRITING INSTRUCTIONAL OBJECTIVES

STEP ONE — Compare two statements

Read the following two statements and compare the differences between them.

> *(1) The purpose of the class period is to help the students learn how to use a Bible Concordance.*

> *(2) At the end of the session the students should be able to use a Bible Concordance to find five familiar passages of scripture related to the concept "covenant."*

Some questions to consider:

> What differences have you identified?
> Which statement is more general than the other?
> Which statement is more directed to student activity?
> Which statement would be more helpful after the session to guide the teacher in evaluating whether or not the objective was achievedI

Statement two (2) is the better of the two because it is more specific, more focused on student activity, and more helpful for later evaluation.

STEP TWO — Compare two more statements

Read the following two statements and compare them.

> *(1) At the end of the session the students should be able to **list** six different actions and/or teachings of both Amos and Jeremiah and to **compare** the differences and and similarities between them.*

> *(2) At the end of the session the students should be able to **understand** some of the important teachings of the prophets Amos and Jeremiah.*

Some questions to consider:

> What do you notice about these two statements when you compare them?
> Which objective states actions of the students that can be seen or heard?
> Which objectives would be more helpful in evaluating the students' achievements?

The first (1) statement is the better of the two because it states in observable terms what a student is expected to do.

A Summary Statement

The above two sets of examples of objectives focus on the two primary, essential criteria for writing objectives; (1) written for students in terms of their action and (2) written with students actions that can be observed — we can see and/or hear what the students do. Whenever writing objectives these two elements should always be included.

There are two other criteria which help make objectives more specific and achievable; the **conditions** under which they will be achieved and the **quality** of achievement expected by the teacher. These two aspects of objectives will sharpen them, but may not be included in every objective a teacher writes.

STEP THREE — Two Additional Criteria for Writing Objectives

    A.   The conditions by which objectives will be achieved include time, materials, resources, and in the following objectives the **conditions** are printed in **bold**.

        *(1) By using a **Bible Dictionary** and **commentary (given 30 minutes time)** students should be able to write a two paragraph interpretation of Psalm 23 in their own words.*

        *(2) Given an **unlabeled map** of the lands of the Bible the students should be able to locate accurately all the following places: Dead Sea, Jordan River, Egypt, Sea of Galilee and the Sinai Peninsula.*

    B.   The **quality** with which objectives will be achieved say something of the level of expectation that a teacher has. In the following objectives the words which indicate **quality** are printed in **bold**.

        *(1) By using a Bible dictionary and commentary (given 30 minutes time) the students should be able to write a **two paragraph** interpretation of Psalm 23 in **their own words**.*

        *(2) Given an unlabeled map of the lands of the Bible the students should be able to locate **accurately all** the following places . . . . .*

STEP FOUR — Practice Writing Your Own Objectives

Use the following Main Idea as a basis for writing a set of objectives.

    "Jesus called persons to become his disciples. Twelve men were specifically chosen to learn from and work with Jesus. Jesus needs disciples today to learn from him and work for love, peace, and justice."

Write several objectives based upon the above Main Idea:

At the end of the session the students should be able to:

1.

2.

3.

4.

CHAPTER FIVE

FOCUS ON TEACHING–LEARNING ACTIVITIES

Once the **key concepts** are focused and the **instructional objectives** determined, the teacher should have a clear sense of direction. The next step in planning is to design the **teaching activities** that will most effecitvely communicate the concepts and achieve the objectives. The accent is upon **activity**.

Often a teacher begins his preparation by asking himself, "What am I going to say to the class about the concept of 'covenant'?" That is the wrong question because answering it leads the teacher to think about what he is going to **tell the students.** A more appropriate question would be "What are the students and I going **to do** about the concept of 'covenant'?"

Answering this question leads directly to thinking about activities, what persons will be doing in the classroom to learn.

Teaching activities are defined as all those actions of students and teachers in the classroom. There are many dozens of possible teaching activities that can be organized into several categories as illustrated by the diagram below.

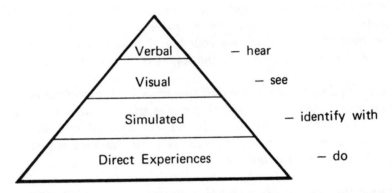

Verbal — hear

Visual — see

Simulated — identify with

Direct Experiences — do

Verbal Activities have been the most common means used in teaching. Teaching activities in this category are: lecture, discussion, recording, sermon, story, reading, and any other type of verbal presentation that depends primarily upon the hearing of the learner. The evidence is that most people do not learn well just by hearing something. In order to be effective, verbal activities must be accompanied by other types of experiences. Hearing for most persons is a passive activity not requiring much participation from the learner. Also, hearing is very selective. We tend to hear what we want to hear.

Another category of teaching activities is the use of visual symbols. **Visual symbols** involve the learner through his sense of seeing. Activities in this category are: use of teaching pictures, filmstrips, map study, seeing movies, looking at books, and many other types of visual presentations. Most persons learn more from what they see than from what they hear. Seeing is less passive than hearing. Seeing elicits a response from the one who sees. When verbal and visual symbols are used together in a combined activity, the learning is more effective than when either is used separately.

Simulated Experiences move us a step farther than verbal and visual activities. To simulate is to act out, to act as if it is real but it is not actually real. Teaching activities in this category are role playing, dramatics, simulation games, some field trips, some creative writing and other experiences which place students in the position of acting out particular feelings, problems, or issues. An example of a creative writing simulated experience would be where a student assumes the role of Moses at the time he has returned to Egypt to seek freedom for the Hebrew slaves. Moses has confronted Pharoah, who has refused to let the people go and instead has increased their work load. Pharoah is uncooperative. The Hebrew people are angry at Moses and Moses wonders whether or not God is going to keep his promise. That is the situation to be simulated. The students are directed to write a letter, as Moses would write, to his wife, father-in-law or friend back in Midian. In doing this assignment one student addressed his letter, "Dear Sheep . . ." A simulated activity involves the students more significantly in developing and identifying with the concepts of the session.

Direct Experiences are those activities when students are actually involved in "for real" situations, problems, and concepts. Because so many concepts in religious teaching tend to be abstract it is often difficult to design direct experience teaching activities.

An example in working on the concept of "love your neighbor as yourself" would be for the students to visit a Convalescent Home or other shut-ins to share with persons some moments of friendship and joy.

We can talk about "love your neighbor" in a long discussion and chances are it will make little impression. We could select pictures from magazines to illustrate examples of persons loving other persons and the meaning would be more memorable. We could act out or write endings to several open-ended stories illustrating persons needing love and this gets closer to the meaning of the concept. And, we could go as a class, or in small groups, to visit some persons who really need love from a neighbor. Which activity would require the most involvement on the part of the students? Which activity would be most memorable? My hunch is that visiting some shut-ins could be remembered by some students for a life-time. Also, the next time the students hear "and you shall love your neighbor as yourself" they will have a specific experience to use as a frame of reference for relating to the concepts of love and neighbor.

The more our teaching activities are in the direction of verbal symbols the less involved the students are and the less they will learn. The more our teaching moves toward direct and simulated experiences the more that a student will be involved in his own learning. Teaching activities at the verbal level tend to restrict the participation and learning of many students. Whereas, teaching activities involving direct experiences tend to include all the students in one way or another.

We suggested earlier that a teacher begin his planning by asking, "What are the students and I going to do?" There is another helpful question a teacher could ask: "What direct experience will best communicate the concept I want to teach?" Direct experiences will not always be thought of, nor are they always feasible or appropriate. Then we should consider what simulated experiences are possible. Verbal activities should be employed only after other activities have been used. Verbal activities should never be used exclusively for a whole instructional period for any age group. It is best when there is a variety of activities in a session involving all the students through several senses.

Deciding which teaching activity to use is the necessary task all teachers must perform.

Here are some criteria that may be used in deciding which teaching activities to employ:

1.   The activity should involve most of the students in an active way.

2.   It should be an activity in which the teacher has some confidence.

3.   It should allow for maximum creativity on the part of the students.

4.   It should not be so familiar as to bore the students.

5. If it is a new activity, students should have the opportunity to experiment with it in order to discover its possibilities.

6. There should usually be a variety of activities offered so that students can have a choice.

7. The activity should contribute directly to communicating the key concepts and achieving the specific objectives.

8. The activity should lead the students to seek answers, state conclusions or express creative responses.

9. Whatever activities are designed should be appropriate to the ages and skills of the students involved.

By using these criteria, teachers should be able to design teaching activities that will involve the students in the active process of their own learning.

Ideas or suggestions for possible teaching activities come from many sources:

** the teacher's manual
** other teachers
** past experiences
** training events

** educational magazines, journals, books
** public-school teachers

Teachers need always to be alert to new ways of designing teaching activities. By reading, sharing, and experiencing a variety of activities teachers will become more resourceful in their planning and teaching.

SAMPLES OF WAYS TO ORGANIZE TEACHING-LEARNING ACTIVITIES

Every lesson plan has a beginning, middle, and end. There are many alternative activities that are appropriate for beginning, developing and ending a lesson. In what follows there are several parts of the typical lesson plan that are identified specifically.

1. **Opening the Session** — The first thing that teachers and students do in a session is one of the most important activities of the whole hour. The opening segment could be as brief as one minute or as long as ten minutes.

2. **Presenting the Subject** — Before students can engage in purposeful study it is helpful to present to them some of the basic information related to the concepts to be developed in the session.

3. **Exploring the Subject** — Students are more motivated for learning when they are able to work individually or in small groups to explore further the subject matter that is the focus of the day's session.

4. **Responding Creatively** — Learning is reinforced and students are able to express themselves in meaningful ways when they are encouraged to respond in one or more creative ways to what they have learned.

5. **Concluding the Session** — Each session should be brought to a fitting conclusion so that students sense a completeness to the sequence of learning activities experienced that day.

All teacher's manuals include the above five categories whether or not they are identified by the same titles. Even though there is something of a logical sequence to these five parts of a lesson plan it is possible that the Presenting, Exploring and Responding activities could be experienced in a variety of combinations. It is possible that Presenting and Exploring activities could happen simultaneously as when students are researching a subject using a variety of resources. Also, Exploring and Responding activities may happen together as when students are writing their own script for selected frames of a filmstrip.

There are many, many different teaching-learning activities that can be used in each of the above five parts of a lesson plan.

Some Ways to Open the Session

- Students read a definition of a concept and state questions.

- Teacher reads a story or passage of scripture and asks questions.

- Students listen to a recording: song, story, commentary or other prerecorded material.

- Students view a film or filmstrip which introduces subject.

- Teacher and students look at and discuss a photo or painting.

- Students select a passage of scripture or concept to explore further.

- Teacher refers to recent school, church, or community events.

- Teacher and students brainstorm a subject.

- Teachers involve students in a voting activity.

- Teacher uses a newspaper or magazine article or photo.

- (add your own)

Some Ways to Present the Subject

- Teacher make a brief presentation (lecture).

- Students read a selection from scripture or other resource book.

- Students view a film or filmstrip.

- Students listen to tape recording of a story, sermon, scripture, commentary, report, etc.

- Students present brief reports that are previously prepared.

- Guest speaker or other resource persons could present subject through lecture, interview, panel, debate, etc.

- Teacher reads or tells a story.

— Teacher or students present a puppet play.

— Teacher involves students in a values clarification strategy.

— Students go on a field trip.

— (add your own).

Some Ways to Explore the Subject

— Students do research in Bible and/or other resource books.

— Students write scripts for filmstrips, slides, puppet plays or other dramas.

— Students use photos or other materials to select visual expressions of a concept.

— Students interview other persons and record interview.

— Students discuss with teacher and other students.

— Students use prepared worksheets.

— Students select a learning center in which to work.

— Students participate in a simulation game.

— Students listen to prerecorded resources.

— Students do a values clarification strategy.

— (add your own).

Some Ways to Respond Creatively

— Writing activities (letters, reports, poems, newspapers, scripts, etc.)

— Write-on slide, filmstrip and film activities.

— Recording activities (news reports, scripts, songs, dramas, interviews, etc.).

— Drama activities (role play, puppets, dance, pantomime, drama, etc.).

— Construction activities (scale models, maps, three-dimensional objects).

— Painting or drawing activities.

— Photography activities (slides, photos, 8 mm films, polaroid camera).

— Collage (felt and burlap, natural materials, junk, photos, etc.).

— Multi-media activities.

— (add your own).

Some Ways to Conclude the Session

— Each student shares his creativity.

— Teacher leads discussion in which students express their own ideas.

— Teacher and/or students prepare for time of worship.

— Teacher summarizes.

— Students write completion of open-ended sentences.

— Teacher and/or students close with prayer.

— Teacher and students sing song together.

— Whole class meditates in silence for one minute.

— Students lead a time of celebration.

— Students decide on a project or action for next week.

— (add your own).

PRACTICE FOCUSING ON TEACHING-LEARNING ACTIVITIES

Following is a series of activities that you could participate in to help you in the process of focusing on teaching-learning activities.

Activity One

Look at your teacher's manual.
Read all the material for one unit.
Write down on a blank sheet of paper all the activities that are suggested for the unit.
Categorize all the activities according to Verbal, Visual, Simulated or Direct experiences.

Activity Two

Add another step to the above activity.
Categorize all the activities according to the five parts of a lesson plan: Opening, Presenting, Exploring, Responding and Closing.

Activity Three

Read again the ten suggestions under each of the above five parts of a lesson.
In the blank to the left of each suggestion place a check mark (✔) for each time you have used the activity in the last six weeks.
If an item has three or more ✔ 's you may be using that activity too often.

Activity Four

Use the ten suggestions for five parts of the lesson again.
In the blank place a circle (O) for each activity you have never used before.
If you have three or more O's for one of the parts it may be that you are overlooking a very valuable activity.
Some of the activities are developed in greater detail in this manual. If any of the following subjects have O's you may want to read more in this manual or in other books listed in the Bibliography to help you gain information and confidence to try a new activity.

** Uses of Media: Including slides, filmstrips, cassette recordings, films and overhead projection.

** Values Clarification Strategies

** Asking Questions and Leading Discussion

** Creative Activities.

Activity Five

Read the ten suggestions for five parts of a lesson once more. Put an (X) next to each of the suggestions you intend to include in your next unit of teaching.

CHAPTER SIX

FOCUS ON TEACHING-LEARNING RESOURCES

Teaching-learning **activities** are what teachers and students **do** in and out of the classroom to experience and communicate particular concepts. **Resources** are what teachers and students **use** in the process of teaching and learning.

Resources may be organized in the same categories as described in the preceding section on teaching-learning activities. Some example of resources in each category are:

Resources for VERBAL Activities

— cassette tapes to listen to
— cassette recorder for recording students' statements
— phonograph player for listening to records
— pens or pencils and paper for writing activities
— resource books without diagrams, maps or photos with just words

Resources for VISUAL Activities

— maps, charts, posters, photographs and banners
— filmstrips and projectors
— overhead projector and transparencies
— 16mm films and projectors
— 8mm cameras, films and projectors
— chalk board, bulletin board, white board
— books with photographs, paintings, diagrams, maps
— magazine pictures
— 35mm cameras, slides, projectors
— write-on slides, filmstrips, and films
— flannel board, magnetic board

Resources for SIMULATED Activities

— puppets and stage for puppet plays
— directions and supplies for simulation games
— scripts, props, costumes, etc., for dramas
— materials for constructing some scale models
— resources for motivating, presenting and responding in ways that help students identify with a person, event, or concept

Resources for DIRECT EXPERIENCE Activities

— All the above resources could be used to help students do something directly related to key concept that is connected with his own life experience.
— In addition there are many, many resources that can help students experience learning directly.

Teachers gather resources from many places: closets at home, cupboards at church, local stores, denominational offices and publishers, and even the trash can.

Resources can be as costly as a video-tape system and as inexpensive as a magazine.

If students are to be motivated to become involved in the process of their learning and if they are to use more than verbal symbols to express themselves, then teachers need to use a wide variety of resources.

Resources are as necessary to teaching and learning as dishes and utensils are to eating. You can survive without resources — but not without experiencing considerable frustration.

The same criteria used for determining which teaching activities to employ in the classroom may be used to decide which resources to use.

There are many books, magazines, and articles that suggest creative uses of a wide variety of resources; for instance, every teacher has used teaching pictures in one way or another.

Many teachers have experienced great excitement and satisfaction as they have become involved with other teachers in brainstorming possible ways to use a particular resource.

TEACHER SURVIVAL *

Most teachers can recall vividly the first time they faced a class of students as the TEACHER. For some of us that was a frightening experience. I can remember my first teaching assignment. The Assistant Pastor recruited me to teach a Junior High class. He handed me a Teacher's Manual and a Student's Book, directed me to the room, showed me where to find the light switch, and said, "Good Luck!"

Quite soon I discovered that the Teacher's Manual and Student's Book were not sufficient for the task of planning to teach. I needed what all teachers need, a wide variety of resources and skills from which to select the most appropriate for a particular session. In addition to having resources available, I needed to develop some criteria for determining which resources were of highest priority and most valuable.

What follows is a simple Simulation Game to help teachers approach the business of considering the value of particular resources and setting priorities for their use. The "game" is played most profitably by four or more persons.

WORKSHEET NEEDED

In preparation for playing the game, prepare copies of the worksheet, on page 27, for all players. Note the "contingencies."

THE SITUATION

You have moved to a remote area. (Any place where you feel isolated or alone may be remote.) A neighbor has discovered that you taught church school in the community from which you came. This new community in which you live does not have a church school class, and you are asked to begin one. You agree to teach, but you realize that you need some resources in order to do an effective job.

Since a friend is coming for a visit, you ask him to bring the twelve items listed on the worksheet (page 27). On the way his automobile breaks down. He is going to continue the trip by bus, but he cannot bring all of the resources you requested. Your friend calls long distance, and in three minutes you have to decide which items are most necessary and which items you can manage without. He can bring some items, but he is not sure how many. He will bring as many as he can, based on the order of priority **you** establish. (See page 28 for the next step.)

*TEACHER SURVIVAL by Donald L. Griggs, Copyright, 1970, The Arizona Experiment. Used by permission. TEACHER SURVIVAL is a Simulation Game that can be used by one or more persons to focus on the relative value they place on a variety of teaching-learning resources.

TEACHER SURVIVAL WORKSHEET

THE RESOURCES

In three minutes rank the following items in the order of their priority of importance to you. Rank the most important item as "1" and the least important "12" and everything in between "2" through "11".

Five copies of GOOD NEWS FOR MODERN MAN
—— A translation of the New Testament in today's English.

Creative Activities Kit
—— A box of materials of your choice.

Complete set of Teacher's Manuals and Student's Books
—— from any curriculum you may choose.

A copy of CREATIVE TEACHING IN THE CHURCH
—— A book by Morrison and Foster.

Phonograph and five records —
May include music, songs, narrations, or stories.

One set of Pictures, Posters, Photos, and Maps —
—— Any combination of 20 items.

—— A Hymnal for children and youth.

Tape recorder plus five blank one-hour tapes — could be
—— small portable cassette recorder.

A box of old magazines —
—— any combination of LIFE, TIME, NATIONAL GEOGRAPHIC.

Five each of Children's editions of BIBLE DICTIONARY,
—— ATLAS, ENCYCLOPEDIA.

—— An overhead projector, with materials needed for using it.

Filmstrip/slide Projector with 5 filmstrips, scripts, records, and
—— 100 miscellaneous slides.

SOME CONTINGENCIES

This is a Simulation Game, a small segment of reality. Do not attempt to make every factor of the game fit a real situation. To assist your playing of the game, consider the following:

1. You do have a personal copy of the Bible (Revised Standard Version).

2. You will be teaching this class for an indefinite period of time.

3. The age group of the class is whatever you decide.

4. For the purposes of the game, the resources will be available only if they are delivered to you. (You cannot depend upon gathering a box of old magazines from the neighbors.)

5. Do not consider how large the items are or how much they weigh.

6. For items like filmstrips, records, materials for creative activities, etc., you can imagine any specific titles or materials you would want to have.

NEXT STEP

After you have ranked the above items by yourself, you are informed that two other persons are going to work with you in teaching the class. It just so happens that those persons are with you at the time of the phone call. Now they must participate with you in deciding on one priority list of the resources you need in order to teach.

Work with two or three other persons. You have fifteen minutes in which to arrive at a priority list for your group. Some suggestions that may help:

— Determine which age group is your frame of reference.

— Avoid decisions based on a mathematical average.

— Consider the reasons why another person has ranked items high or low.

— Be flexible and willing to change.

— And be positive about your rationale for ranking the items as you did.

AFTER PLAYING THE GAME

REFLECTION AND DISCUSSION

What follows are some ideas and suggestions for the leader of the session as he guides the group in a period of reflection and discussion. The primary values of using the game in a training event are derived from the interaction of the group with each other, with the leader, and with the game.

When all the groups have finished deciding on their priority lists, plan twenty to thirty minutes for discussion. As groups are finishing at different times, this is a good place for a coffee break. Also, tabulate each group's rankings on a large chart, an overhead transparency, or a chalkboard.

The first question to consider is: "What were the factors that influenced the decisions you made when you were ranking the items by yourself?"

There will be a variety of responses:

1. AGE of the Students
   Some items will be more appropriate for one age group than another. For instance: Bible Atlas, Dictionary, and Encyclopedia may not be high priority for teachers of younger children.

2. NEEDS of the Teacher
   Items such as Teacher's Manuals, **Creative Teaching in the Church** and other books may be ranked high by persons feeling the need of suggestions, outlines, or plans for teaching.

3. VERSATILITY of Resources
   A Tape Recorder, with blank tapes, provides more flexibility in classroom use than a Phonograph. A box of old magazines can be used in a wide variety of ways; whereas a set of teaching pictures or posters may be more limiting. With old magazines a teacher can create his own posters or teaching pictures.

4. USEFULNESS to the Students
   Resources such as the Creative Activities Kit, Tape Recorder, Old Magazines, and GOOD NEWS FOR MODERN MAN can be used by the students in pursuing and expressing their own learning and interests. These allow for considerable involvement by the students.

5. SKILLS of the Teacher
   A teacher who has no skill in reading music or leading singing is not likely to place the HYMNAL high in his priority list. Also, a teacher with considerable skill in music may not place the HYMNAL high because of his ability to teach songs and lead singing without a hymnbook. Other items may suggest similar responses by teachers with different skills.

6. EXPERIENCE of the Teacher
   Some teachers have had wide experience with specific resources and have discovered their value in teaching. If a teacher has often used a tape recorder in his teaching, and experienced success, he is likely to place it high on his priority list. With the same reasoning a person who has never used a tape recorder is likely to place it low.

We have considered six factors which may have influenced a person as he was choosing which items to place high and low on his priority list. There may be other factors that will emerge in the discussion.

IMPLICATIONS FOR PLANNING

One can see quickly that these factors influence teachers all the time. When teachers approach their planning of specific lessons, they use or disregard suggestions in the Teacher's Manual, or then innovate from their own resourcefulness, according to their conscious or unconscious consideration of many of the above factors. Consider briefly the situation of team-teaching in a particular class. When two or more persons are together they bring with them to their planning and teaching different experiences, needs, skills, attitudes, and approaches to teaching. Many breakdowns in the team-teaching process are a result of persons' assuming that others share the same points of view when in fact they may represent great difference.

Perhaps participating in a process of decision-making and discussion similar to the Teacher Survival Simulation Game would help persons focus on their unique skills and needs. When facing these differences at the beginning of their teaching together, it may be possible for them to come to a mutual understanding of each one's place and potential in the planning and teaching process. Often when persons discuss the reasons for making their choices in the Simulation Game, they discover something from other persons that influence them to adjust the items they place high or low on the priority list.

USING TEACHER SURVIVAL GAME IN TEACHER EDUCATION

By participating in the Teacher Survival Simulation Game, persons are helped to:

1. Consider a wider variety of resources for teaching rather than limiting themselves to the familiar items they most often use.

2. Weigh the value of several items over others when choices must be made between them.

3. Hear the values placed on some resources by other persons with different skills, interests, and needs.

4. Participate in the process of decision-making and priority-setting with other persons who may share similar as well as different points of view.

The game can be used successfully as the initial training experience of a new group or staff of teachers. By using the game, persons are involved immediately in the process. The task of ranking the twelve items can be easily accomplished by both experienced and inexperienced teachers.

As a result of making decisions and discussing their implications, teachers face quickly some of the key factors involved in planning and teaching. The experience of playing TEACHER SURVIVAL can be followed by a series of training events that focus more specifically on the procedures of planning, the implementation of resources, the skills of classroom interaction and the content of teaching session.

Local users of the game should experiement with developing their own resource lists. Included might be items readily available in a given church or locality — or they might be items a planning group hopes to introduce to the players.

THE RECYCLE GAME

What follows was first designed for use in a teacher education event. However, the concept of recycling resources is so important for teachers to consider it is suggested that if you are reading this book by yourself you plan for a time when you could play this game, or parts of it, with three or more persons whom you have invited to meet with you.

For a long time persons have been recycling available resources for teaching in the church. When Jesus focused the attention of the people on sheep, a father and two sons, a house built on rock and other familiar objects he was recycling common, available resources to communicate something of what he understood about life, man, and God. To recycle something is to use it over again in a new way to serve other purposes than what was its original intention.

Recycling is an "in" process these days, with emphasis on saving the environment. And, RECYCLE* is also a publication by Dennis Benson that each month describes thirty to forty different recycled resources and processes. The more I considered the concept of recycling and tried recycling some resources myself, the more I became convinced that teachers in the church needed to develop a mind-set that encourages them to employ the recycling process in their planning for teaching. As a result of this interest I developed a workshop design that involves teachers in experiences of recycling.

Step One   Introduce the concept of recycling with some examples and illustrations.

Step Two   Distribute samples of RECYCLE periodical by Dennis Benson or some facsimile copies that have been reproduced. (Dennis will send sample copies on request.)

Step Three   Divide large group into smaller groups of three to six persons. Give each group one of the following items, or let them select from the items:

    **   a bowl of mixed fruit
    **   a loaf of bread (unsliced)
    **   a jug of cold water
    **   a package of food like cookies, cereal, pretzels, potato chips, or others
    **   a bag of mixed candy
    **   a bowl or bag of nuts

Allow groups fifteen minutes to decide on one or more ways their "resource" could be used to help students focus on a biblical-theological concept.

Groups should prepare to present their ideas as quickly as possible.

Spend as much time as necessary to hear from each group. Also, the groups may want to involve the others in experiencing what they have planned.

Use the food as a part of the refreshment break.

Step Four   Repeat the above process, only with different items which may include:

    **   a children's game
    **   a child's toy

*RECYCLE, Dennis Benson, editor. Available from RECYCLE, P.O. Box 12811, Pittsburgh, PA 15241. Nine issues for $5.50. Send for sample copy.

<pre>
**   a magazine
**   a newspaper
**   a football
**   a wallet or purse
**   some empty cartons of various sizes
**   a suitcase
**   a Sears catalog
**   wrist watch or alarm clock
</pre>

In this period persons would have up to a half hour to prepare a way to use the resource as part of a larger strategy for a classroom session.

If a spirit duplicator is available, it is very helpful to the whole group for the small groups to write up their strategy on a spirit master to duplicate and distribute to everyone present. This way each person will be able to take home with him as many plans as there are groups.

Step Five   Distribute copies of the **Bible** or **Good News for Modern Man.** Have a few Concordances available also.

Instruct persons to spend five to ten minutes locating a verse or passage of scripture that illustrates the concept of recycling.

Each person shares his passage with the whole group or a smaller group.

Step Six   This is the closing experience of the workshop. Encourage persons to complete the statement, "Recycling is . . ." These statements then become the parts of a litany. To each of the statements the whole group could respond with "Thank you, God, for your creative spirit."

FLYING THE FRIENDLY SKIES TO A.E.C.T. *

I am 37,000 feet somewhere between San Francisco and Philadelphia as I am writing copy for the June issue of MEDIALOG. Five hours without interruption from the telephone is a good time for thinking and writing. I am on my way to the A.E.C.T. Convention in Atlantic City where I will spend several days previewing the latest equipment and material resources in the audio visual and media field. A.E.C.T. (Association for Educational Communication and Technology) is a national association of professional educators and media specialists in public education, business, government, and religious education. About 10,000 of these folk gather each year at the national convention.

As in other years I can expect to meet many exciting persons who are working hard at improving the quality of education. I will see hundreds of commercial exhibits displaying everything from pens and pencils to the sophisticated closed-circuit, color, videotape systems. Films, filmstrips, tapes, books, and other media will be available by the hundreds for preview and purchase. Workshops, seminars, and multi-media presentations will happen hour after hour. I feel like the child trying to decide between the circus and the toy store when I enter the halls of the convention.

MINI MEDIA "CONVENTIONS" IN YOUR AREA

I have just described a media convention I will be attending and I know this is something that is not possible for most church teachers. However, if you are interested in media — in the resources available, in the comparable features of several types or brands of projectors, recorders, screens, etc., in the use of media in the classroom, then there are some things you can do in your area to gain some of the benefits of a "convention."

1. A.E.C.T. has regional and state organizations that may conduct a conference or convention near your home. They are usually open to visitors. Contact your school district media specialist for information.

2. Regional offices of church denominations and ecumenical organizations are beginning to establish Media Resource Centers. Contact your denomination's education office to inquire whether or not such a center is nearby. A Media Resource Center is a great place to browse, to consult with the coordinator, and to preview resources.

3. Most local school districts and county education offices have Instructional Materials Centers or Media Resource Centers. Even though the resources are intended for public school instruction you would be amazed at how much you can learn from a visit to such a Center. Sometimes it is possible to arrange to borrow resources or equipment to use in your own classroom.

4. School libraries are changing. In some of the newer schools where there is an emphasis on open space, individualizing instruction, and learning contracts there is provision for a library or resource center where students have access to a wide variety of media equipment and materials. Visit such a school to observe the students in action. It is possible you will find some good ideas to implement in your classroom.

5. Plan with teachers from several other churches to have a "mini-media convention" in your own town. Each teacher could bring the following ten items to share with the others. Ten

*Reprinted from original material that appeared in the June 1974 issue of CHURCH TEACHERS.

teachers times ten items means each teacher may be introduced to 90 new media resources. Then, don't stop there; arrange for a way that you can borrow from each other and continue to share your new findings.

The ten items to bring are:

- 2 favorite filmstrips

- 2 new students' resource or reading books

- 1 best teacher's manual

- 1 most-used media equipment

- 2 favorite records or tapes

- 2 activities the students enjoy

What an exciting time you could have with some other teachers as you experience your own "mini-media convention."

Don't wait for someone else to start it. Get it started yourself. Let us know how it turns out.

GIMMICKS AND GADGETS VS. CREATIVE USE OF RESOURCE

Teachers are as much a target for educational marketing specialists as children are for the toy manufacturers. There is always something new being promoted as the newest, best, easiest to use, most successful whatever. In our desire to motivate students and to increase our effectiveness it is not surprising that we are **sold** the latest gadget or gimmick. (I have a cupboard full of such purchases.) But, we need to keep in mind several concerns as we consider buying or using a new resource, technique, or piece of equipment:

1. Will I be able to use **it** (the resource, technique, or equipment) more than once? We do not have enough money to be able to afford one-time use of anything. It is much more valuable if **it** can be used several times in a variety of ways.

2. Does **it** supplement the curriculum I am using or do I have to dispense with my curriculum? A resource is much more valuable if I can use it to supplement the given curriculum.

3. Is the resource primarily for me or for the student? Ordinarily the resource is worth more if it is something that engages the student's interest and involvement. I need some resources too, but if I have to choose between something for me or something for the students I will seldom be wrong if I choose in the student's favor.

4. Does the resource come with a manual, user's guide, or outline of suggested uses? I can be sure the resource will be used more often and more effectively if the producers, authors, or manufacturers have offered a helpful list of practical, easy to use suggestions or procedures.

5. Does the resource encourage student exploration, involvement, and creativity? If students can remain passive when using the resource then it is not as valuable as when students must be actively engaged with the resource.

By considering these questions and others we may be able to avoid being sold a gadget or gimmick that looks attractive and promising but ends up being just another disappointment. When we carefully assess the value of a new resource, technique, or piece of equipment and consider the many ways it can be used effectively as part of our teaching then it becomes a very valuable creative resource that is worth whatever it costs.

IT IS NOT A QUESTION OF WHETHER TO USE MEDIA OR NOT, BUT RATHER, WHICH MEDIA. A lecture is one type of media and a field trip is another. Reading about Jerusalem is a medium using the printed word, seeing a filmstrip or movie showing Jerusalem is a visual medium, and interviewing a person who has visited Jerusalem is a more personalized way of discovering Jerusalem.

TEACHERS ARE THE MOST VALUABLE RESOURCE

When we have budgeted money for church education, built classrooms, purchased equipment, selected a curriculum and arranged for a schedule we have contributed much to creating an effective church education program. However, the most valuable resource for teaching has not been mentioned yet — the teacher. It doesn't make much difference which curriculum, how many filmstrips, or how many square feet of floor space per student if we have not recognized that the most critical factor determining the success of church education is the teacher. Teachers do what no curriculum or media resource will ever be able to do — smile, laugh, relate, show interest and surprise, love, forgive, touch, cry, pray, shout, whisper, and . . . . .

CHAPTER SEVEN
PRACTICE THE PLANNING PROCESS

In the previous four chapters we have discussed four of the essential components to the planning process.

First, we considered the key concepts to be focused upon in a session or unit. This is one way to respond to the question "What am I going to teach?"

Second, we compared the differences between general goals and specific instructional objectives concluding that determining objectives for teaching is crucial to the planning process. This is a way to answer the question "What will the students learn?"

Third, we focused on four different levels of teaching activities with the observation that there are many, many different activities that can be selected for involving students in learning. In this chapter we responded to the question "What teaching activities will I plan for the session?"

Fourth, we identified a wide variety of resources that are available that can be used by teachers and students to make teaching and learning a very involving and interesting experience. The question, "What resources will the students and I use?", was considered in this chapter.

When you put it all together it is like building a bridge.

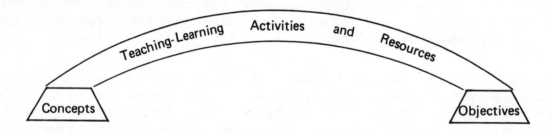

The teaching activities and resources could be just "busy-work" if they are not directly connected to the concepts we want to communicate and the objectives we want to achieve.

In order to put into practice this process of planning, teachers are encouraged to use the materials on the following pages. There are instructions for each step and a worksheet provided. It works best if you can do this activity with at least one other person. The instructions suggest you plan for just one session. However, if you have time you may want to plan for two or three more sessions to complete a unit of study.

PRACTICE THE PLANNING PROCESS

Introduction You are a teacher of a class of students. Determine for yourself the age of your students. You meet with your class for one hour each week. Next week's lesson begins a new unit on **Jesus' Disciples, Then and Now.** Following you will notice a lot of suggestions of what you could use in your teaching. You cannot teach everything. You must start someplace. So, select what you want to teach in your first session.

Step One Select the **main ideas** you want to focus on in Session One. **Write them on the worksheet.**

A. Jesus called twelve men to become his apostles.

B. Other persons who learned from Jesus and followed him were called disciples.

C. A disciple is a person who follows and learns from someone else. The word is used in the New Testament of the followers of John the Baptist and Paul, but especially of the followers of Jesus.

D. Peter, Andrew, James, John, Thomas, Matthew, Judas, and five other men were the twelve apostles.

E. The apostles continued Jesus' ministry after his death.

F. In the Book of the Acts of the Apostles there are many accounts of the work the apostles did to establish the Church.

G. The apostles had difficulties in understanding Jesus' work and teachings and many times asked him questions, were unfaithful in their following, or argued among themselves.

H. The apostles were very enthusiastic about and committed to the work Jesus called them to do and many times spoke and acted fearlessly.

I. Jesus needs disciples to serve him today by speaking and acting in the world to bring love, peace, justice and health to mankind.

J. There are persons today who are acting like the disciples in the early church.

K. The problems and circumstances of today are in many ways similar to those in the days of the first disciples.

L. (Write your own.)

Step Two   Select the **objectives** that are appropriate for the main ideas you have already selected. **Write them on the worksheet.**

AT THE END OF THE SESSION THE STUDENTS SHOULD BE ABLE TO:

A.   **Define** in their own words the meaning of disciple, apostle, called, learn, and follow.

B.   **Name** the twelve apostles that Jesus chose.

C.   **Identify** four of the apostles and **describe** several important characteristics or actions of each.

D.   **Explain** the difference between disciple and apostle.

E.   **Locate** three places in the New Testament where the twelve apostles are listed.

F.   **Locate** at least six passages of scripture that **describe** some of the actions of the apostles and disciples.

G.   **Describe** some of the problems the disciples had in following Jesus.

H.   **Identify** with the feelings the disciples had when they learned that Jesus was crucified.

I.   **Suggest** some examples of ways persons are speaking and acting today as disciples.

J.   **Apply** the meaning of discipleship in the New Testament to the needs of the world today.

K.   **Decide** on several ways they can be disciples in their homes, school, and neighborhood.

L.   (Write your own.)

Step Three   Select **teaching activities** that will help communicate the main ideas and achieve the objectives. Select at least one activity for each of the five parts of the Session: Opening, Presenting, Exploring, Creating, and Concluding. **Write them on your worksheet.**

A. State questions about key concepts and do research in the New Testament and other resource books.

B. Investigate one or more key persons by reading key passages of scripture and other resource books.

C. See filmstrip on the twelve apostles and look for important events, relationships with Jesus, and/or personal experiences and characteristics.

D. Write a script for a filmstrip about the apostles of Jesus.

E. Create slides to illustrate a story about Jesus and the disciples.

F. Listen to or read a story about Jesus and disciples in his day; and in our day.

G. Write a story about experiences persons have in trying to be followers of Jesus.

H. Search in magazines or newspapers to find examples of modern disciples of Jesus.

I. Work on a values clarification strategy of rank order, voting, or values continuum to focus on disciples and discipleship.

J. Use magazines to make a collage or montage, to mount teaching pictures, to photograph for slides, or to do picture lifting for slides or transparencies.

K. Do some informal role play or dramatics.

L. Discuss some situations where disciples are needed today and decide ways to act as disciples.

M. (Make up your own activities.)

Step Four   Select **resources** that are necessary to do the activities that are planned. **Write your own choices on the worksheet.**

A. Copies of the New Testament for each student.

B. Several copies each of **People of the Bible, Young Readers Bible Dictionary, Concise Concordance,** and **Golden Bible Atlas.**

C. Filmstrip: Into All the World, parts I and II. An overview of New Testament persons and events.

D. Overhead projector with all necessary materials and screen.

E. Cassette tape recorder with power cord, microphone, and blank tapes.

F. Write-On Slides or Write-On Filmstrip material with pens and pencils.

G. Box of newspapers and magazines, scissors, glue, and construction paper.

H. Blank paper and felt pens or pencils.

I. Cassette tape recording:
Call of Disciples from "Thesis Tapes," P.O. Box 11724, Pittsburgh, PA 15228.

J. A set of teaching pictures on Jesus and the apostles.

K. Materials to create puppets.

L. (Make up your own resources.)

PLANNING FOR TEACHING

– WORKSHEET –

MAIN IDEAS FOR SESSION ONE

INSTRUCTIONAL OBJECTIVES FOR SESSION ONE
At the end of the session the students should be able to:

TIME	TEACHING ACTIVITIES	RESOURCES
Opening		
Presenting		
Exploring		
Responding Creatively		
Concluding		

A SAMPLE LESSON PLAN

There are many, many ways to plan for teaching. Compare this lesson plan with the one you created. Use the criteria outlined in the next chapter to evaluate both your plan and this sample plan. Compare the similarities and differences between the two plans.

MAIN IDEA

Persons are called by Jesus to become his disciples. Twelve of Jesus' original disciples were identified as Apostles. The twelve Apostles followed and learned from Jesus. Each of the twelve apostles was a unique person.

INSTRUCTIONAL OBJECTIVES

At the end of the session the students should be able to:

1. Define disciple and apostle in their own words.

2. Locate three listings of the twelve apostles in the Gospels.

3. Describe some unique characteristics and actions of one apostle.

4. Express in a creative form their own interpretation of and identification with one apostle.

TIME	TEACHING ACTIVITIES	RESOURCES
Opening	Students read definitions of **disciple** and **apostle** in T.E.V. Word List and Bible Dictionary	T.E.V. New Testaments Young Readers Bible Dictionary
5 mins.		Bible Encyclopedia for Children
	Make listings of endings to	
	"A disciple is . . . . ."	
	"An apostle is . . . . ."	

Presenting the Subject	Ask question: "Who were the 12 disciples specially chosen by Jesus?"	
10 mins.	Write names down. Accept all names suggested. Evaluate later.	Newsprint and felt markers
	Use T.E.V. Index to find lists of disciples' names in three gospels. Compare with original suggestions.	Ditto copies of three lists.

TIME	TEACHING ACTIVITIES	RESOURCES
	Compare the three lists and discuss similarities and differences. (Ditto lists ahead of time to save time.)	Ditto copies of three lists.

Exploring the Subject

15 mins.

Select one disciple and use resources to explore using some of these questions:

1. What does the disciple's name mean?

2. How did he first meet Jesus?

3. What are some special things he did?

4. What kind of person was he?

5. What kind of relationship did he have with Jesus?

Resources:
People of the Bible

Armed With Love

Bible Dictionaries

Bible Encyclopedia for Children

Chart with questions

Responding Creatively

15 min.

Students select one of the three activities to express their learnings and impressions of the disciple they investigated.

1. Write a brief letter introducing yourself as a disciple. Write the letter in the first-person, in the role of the disciple.

   Paper and Pencils

2. Create a set of write-on slides to illustrate some of the memorable characteristics of your disciple or some of the important events in his life.

   Write-On slides, pens, pencils and projector

3. Work with another student, using a tape recorder to create and record an interview with your disciple.

   Cassette tape recorder

Concluding

10 mins.

Share letters, slides, and recordings with the whole class.

Last activity: Complete the sentence, "Disciples are . . . . ."

Use completed sentences as parts of a Litany. Corporate response could be: "Help us God, to follow Jesus and to serve others."

CHAPTER EIGHT

CRITERIA FOR EVALUATING LESSON PLANS

After you have created your practice lesson plan or any other lesson plan you intend to use with your students you could use the following criteria as a basis for evaluating those plans. In the list of criteria you will first read a question that should be asked of your lesson plan, then there is a brief commentary on that question to help you in your evaluation. Also, included, is a reference to another chapter in this manual where you will find further discussion of the principles and skills implied by the question and commentary.

1. *Is the main idea limited to a few key concepts?*

    One of the important aspects of planning for teaching is to limit the number of concepts to be communicated in one session. It is possible for the **teacher** to "cover" a lot of concepts in one session, but it is much more important for the **students** to participate in "uncovering" a few key concepts. Keep the concepts connected to each other and related to the life experiences of the students.

    For review of this subject read again chapter three, "Focus on Key Concepts."

2. *Are the main ideas and objectives appropriate for the age group?*

    With younger students it is more important to select appropriate parts of a story or event than it is to try to teach the whole story. We need to be sure the students have mastered some of the basic skills before expecting them to achieve more complex objectives. With older students we can deal with abstractions and symbols whereas younger students will be more limited by their concrete thinking.

    For review of this subject look over chapters three and four, "Focus on Key Concepts" and "Focus on Instructional Objectives."

3. *Are the main ideas and objectives directly connected?*

    It is not surprising to find situations where main ideas and objectives are not directly related to each other. For instance, teachers often select a main idea related to slavery of the Hebrews in Egypt and then select an objective focusing on contemporary forms and situations of slavery.

    Slavery is the only thing connecting the two, but the historical situations are three thousand years apart. If the main idea of the Hebrews as slaves in Egypt is introduced then the objective should be related to the main idea and not to contemporary forms of slavery. If that objective is intended then a related main idea should be selected. It would be possible to use both main ideas and both objectives even in the same session.

4. *Which types of teaching activities and resources are to be used?*

    In reviewing all the teaching activities and resources that are planned there should be a balance of verbal, visual, simulated and direct experiences. If there is a heavy use of just verbal activities and resources then the plan is out of balance. There needs to be a blending of all the different types of experiences.

Check again on chapters five and six, "Focus on Teaching-Learning Activities" and "Focus on Teaching-Learning Resources."

5. *What kinds of questions did the teachers ask during the session?*

There are at least three categories of questions which include information, analytical and personal questions. All three types of questions should be asked during the session. If there are more information questions than the other two categories, then the students are not being encouraged to think enough and apply the subject matter to their own lives.

For more on the subject of question asking, turn to chapter nine, "The Art of Asking Questions."

6. *What choices did the students get to make during the session?*

Every student should have the opportunity to make a number of choices during the sessions. Students are more motivated and more involved when they are encouraged to make choices during the session. Some choices are a little like deciding which book to read or which colors to use to express a feeling. Other choices may be big, like deciding how to interpret a passage of scripture or deciding how to act in a particular situation. Little or Big, students need many opportunities to make choices.

The subject of student choices is presented in more detail in chapter twelve, "Ways to Increase Student Participation."

7. *Are there a variety of activities and resources planned for the session?*

A one activity lesson is a dull lesson. Students represent different abilities, interests, and needs so that teachers must plan for a variety of activities and resources in order to respond to the individual student differences. Students need a change of pace, they need to build from one activity to the next in order to maintain a high level of motivation.

Read further in chapters ten and twelve, "Creative Uses of Media" and "Ways to Increase Student Participation."

8. *If the students are expected to do something new, have they had a chance to practice or experiment?*

Teachers should regularly introduce new activities and resources for the students to use in their exploring and creating. In order to insure the student's success with new activities and resources, there needs to be a time for practice and experimentation where students can find out for themselves how to do or use what the teacher has planned. The same principle applies to the teacher who plans to use a new resource or try a new activity. There needs to be time allowed for previewing, practicing and experimenting by the teacher.

9. *Has the room been arranged to facilitate the achievement of the intended objectives?*

Arrangement of tables and chairs; placement of learning centers, activity corners and resource equipment; display of visual materials on the wall, bulletin board or chalk board; and easy accessibility of all necessary supplies all contribute significantly to smooth functioning of the class and achievement of the intended objectives. Look at your room before the students arrive. What does the room say to you? It should speak very loudly of what is expected to happen in that sesson. The room arrangement needs to be changed regularly, sometimes as often as weekly.

10. *How much time will be required for each of the activities that is planned?*

The best lesson plan ever can be "shot-down" if sufficient time has not been allowed for each activity. Be realistic about time. Allow enough time for students to work without being rushed. Be flexible enough to adjust the schedule if necessary. Also, plan for some additional activities for those students who work more quickly or have more ability.

By applying these questions to the plans you have made it should be possible to evaluate what you have planned before trying to teach the plan. If you can discuss the plan with someone else you should be able to receive enough feedback for your responses to the questions to be realistic. Consider reworking some of your plans before you enter the classroom to teach them.

CHAPTER NINE

THE ART OF ASKING QUESTIONS

Some of us remember when it was said, "Children should be seen, not heard." Perhaps we also remember teachers we had who did most of the talking. Now we live in a day when we encourage children to express themselves to be heard by adults and when teachers are aware that learning does not occur as much when they do most of the talking. Interaction is basic to communication and learning. Interaction happens when teachers and students express themselves directly and listen to each other attentively. When I ask students to recall their favorite teachers and to reflect on what it was about those teachers that they liked, more often than not the students respond with comments like:

> "They are really interested in what I think and say."
> "They make the subject interesting so that you want to talk about it."
> "They don't make you feel stupid when you give dumb answers."
> "They really listen to me."

All of these comments demonstrate that the students truly appreciate a teacher who has developed some skills in guiding classroom interaction.

This chapter will focus on the skill of asking questions. Perhaps the most important resource for guiding student thinking and learning is **questions.** Questions are the least expensive resource available to us — they only cost the time it takes to plan for or think of them. I dare say it is no exaggeration to conclude that every teacher uses many questions every time he teaches. Questions are very flexible because they can be asked by teachers **and** students.

- Teachers can ask questions to a whole class.
- Teachers can ask a question of one student.
- Questions can be written on worksheets or tests.
- Questions can be used as part of a set of instructions.
- Students can ask questions of teachers.
- Students can ask questions of each other.
- Students can raise questions for their own research.

In addition to the many ways that questions can be asked it is possible to combine questions with a wide variety of teaching-learning activities and resources.

Questions can be used to:

- stimulate a discussion of a familiar subject.
- introduce a new subject.
- review a subject studied previously.
- reflect on some personal experiences.
- connect a biblical subject to some personal experiences.
- interpret a biblical passage.
- motivate further research of a subject.
- evaluate a film, filmstrip, recording, etc.
- probe further into a subject.
- analyze a personal or social problem.
- debrief a simulation game or other activity.

- brainstorm solutions to a problem or issue.
- interview a guest resource person.
- consider possible alternative actions or individuals.
- clarify the values persons express.
- explore beliefs and commitments of persons.

Even though questions are very valuable and can be used in many different ways, questions come in a variety of shapes and sizes. There are several ways that have been used to categorize questions.

1. One educator classifies teacher's questions into four main categories.

    a. COGNITIVE RECALL — questions which simply ask for specific facts gained from reading a book, observing a film or hearing a lecture.
       Example: "What happened to Joseph after his brothers sold him to the caravan?"

    b. CONVERGENT — questions which utilize common information to prove a point or support a generalization.
       Example: "What evidence is there that Joseph . . ."
                "How do you know that . . ."
                "Compare the actions of Joseph with . . ."

    c. DIVERGENT — questions which make use of some known information as a starting point, but the answer moves in some other direction.
       Example: "How would you feel if your brothers sold you and you were taken to a foreign country?"
                "What would happen if . . ."

    d. EVALUATIVE — questions which seek to use known information to reach some kind of a value judgement.
       Example: "Was Joseph right in telling his brothers of the dreams he had?"

2. Another educator classifies teacher and student questions into three general categories:

    a. BIG, PERENNIAL, LIFE-DESTINY, OPEN-ENDED QUESTIONS.
       The answers to these questions involve us in continual debate. The answers must be followed with another question because there never is a final absolute answer.
       Example: "Who am I?"   "Who is God?"   "What is Faith?"

    b. MIDDLE-SIZED, MEANS-ENDS QUESTIONS.
       There are good answers to these questions, but we should put a semi-colon after these answers to symbolize that there is more to learn, the answers are not final.
       Example: "What do you value most?"
                "What does it mean to you to be a Christian?"

    c. SMALL, QUESTIONS OF MEANS.
       Important questions of limited scope seeking information, statement of fact.
       Example: "Where would you look to find the meaning of the word covenant?"

3. I have chosen another way to categorize questions which I identify as the P-A-I approach. Most questions can easily be identified by one of the following three categories.

P — PERSONAL LEVEL OF QUESTIONS

We are not talking about getting personal or invading a person's privacy. Rather, we are referring to questions that are related to a person's own life experience, questions a student can identify with personally. The intent of instruction is to guide students in their personal decision-making and value-forming. Questions at this level are an effective means for engaging students in the process of thinking, reflecting, expressing, and acting on concerns that relate to them personally.

Some examples:
"If **you** had been Moses, what would **you** have done when . . .?"
"What are some times when **you** were asked to do something that was very hard to do?"

A — ANALYTICAL LEVEL OF QUESTIONS

Analytical questions require students **to think** in order to respond. Analytical questions do not assume right answers. Questions of this type are more open, with the potential of many different answers or responses. The same analytical question could be asked of every student in the class, with each giving a different response. Analytical questions ask, "What do you think . . .?" and suggest that the teacher really wants to know what the student thinks, and when he expresses what he thinks his thoughts will be accepted.

Some examples:
"What are some reasons why Moses would be reluctant to return to Egypt?"
"What do you think Moses means when he said . . .?"

I — INFORMATION LEVEL OF QUESTIONS

Information questions require students to **remember something** in order to answer the question. As a result of reading, hearing, or otherwise receiving information, the students are expected to remember some of the facts in order to answer the questions. Information questions are more closed as they tend to assume that there are right answers. Students who are asked a lot of information level of questions often feel like they are being tested. It is almost impossible to have a discussion guided by information questions.

Some examples:
"Where did Moses live as a young child?"
"To what country did Moses flee after killing the Egyptian?"

SOME GENERAL COMMENTS

Too often teachers ask questions without having prepared the questions in advance. Information questions are the easiest to ask, but other than getting a right answer they do not lead very far unless they are followed up with Analytical and Personal questions. Questions are one of the primary means for motivating students to think and express themselves and thereby become more involved in the process of their own learning. Teachers should plan carefully some key Analytical and Personal questions that could be used in the class period to pursue further some of the information that is presented. A balance of questions representing all three levels will guide students and teachers to experience a lot of interaction and learning from each other.

A DISCOVERY IN HAWAII

When I present these three levels of questions in a workshop, I usually start with information questions, then move to Analytical and Personal questions. When I make the presentation I use an overhead projector and write the three key words on a transparency. While doing a workshop in Hawaii I was struck by the three letters P—A—I and had a hunch that those letters may form an Hawaiian word. Hawaiian words have a lot of syllables and in speaking every syllable is pronounced. I suggested that this was a possibility, but no one present knew enough Hawaiian to know for sure whether or not pai was a word. The next day a woman returned to the workshop and presented me with a paper that had a few notes she had copied from an Hawaiian-English dictionary. Sure enough "pai" is an Hawaiian word with many possible meanings. However, the preferred translation of "pai" is: "To stir up, lift up, arouse and excite." What a discovery! Perhaps if teachers were to use a balanced mixture of Personal, Analytical, and Information questions students would really be stirred up, aroused, encouraged, and excited to think, reflect, and express themselves as they are involved in learning activities.

PRACTICE IDENTIFYING AND WRITING THREE LEVELS OF QUESTIONS

STEP ONE: Read Luke 15:11-32

STEP TWO: Classify the following questions according to the three levels (P) Personal, (A) Analytical, (I) Information

  — Who are the three main characters in this parable?

  — Why do you think Jesus told this parable?

  — If you had been the younger son how would you have felt as you were walking back to your father?

  — What feelings do you think the father had when the younger son left home? When he returned home? When the older son inquired about the party?

  — What did the younger son say to himself when he decided to return to his father?

  — What are some times when you have been forgiven by someone? How did you feel?

  — What do you think this parable teaches us about the relationship between God and persons?

STEP THREE: Read Matthew 18:21-35 about the Parable of the Unforgiving Servant. Write two questions to represent each level based on that parable.

    Information   1.

                       2.

    Analytical   1.

                       2.

    Personal   1.

                       2.

STEP FOUR: Compare your questions with another person and evaluate your questions together.

STEP FIVE: Write questions appropriate for the next session you will be teaching.

SOME HELPFUL GUIDELINES FOR ASKING QUESTIONS

1. *ASK QUESTIONS THAT ARE MORE OPEN THAN CLOSED.*

Questions with only one right answer or implying a "yes" or "no" response are more closed. These questions are more a test of memory than they are inquiry into subject matter. When tempted to ask a closed question make a statement instead. Then ask open, analytical, probing questions.

2. *ASK ONLY ONE QUESTION AT A TIME.*

More than one question is confusing to the student. Teachers who ask several questions at once usually have not thought carefully or prepared adequately and are "fishing" for the right question.

3. *PRESENT QUESTIONS TO THE WHOLE CLASS.*

Instead of putting one student "on the spot" by directing a question to him, offer the question to the whole class. By being aware of a student's readiness it is possible to recognize who wants to answer. A student can be called upon to respond without the teacher speaking a word; through eye contact, gesture with the hand, or nod of the head.

4. *PROVIDE FEEDBACK AFTER A STUDENT RESPONDS.*

The teacher can reinforce students and facilitate further discussion by providing verbal and non-verbal feedback so that they will know the teacher has heard and received the response.

5. *AFTER AN INITIAL QUESTION AND RESPONSE, FOLLOW UP WITH PROBING QUESTIONS.*

Probing questions are next questions that follow first questions. Probing questions lead to further inquiry and exploration in depth of a subject. Probing questions can also provide a degree of reinforcement and feedback.

6. *AFTER ASKING A QUESTION BE SILENT.*

The best "next step" after asking a question is to be silent. If the question is clearly stated and if the students have sufficient data with which to answer then they need some time to think. Ten seconds is not too much time. However, ten seconds of silence can feel like an eternity to a teacher who is a little anxious. Leave the burden of the silence on the students. Bite your tongue and relax, usually someone will respond.

7. *USE AN INQUIRY STYLE RATHER THAN AN INTERROGATION STYLE.*

Inquiry is a style or approach that says to the student, "I'm with you; I'm interested in what you think and say." Interrogation puts persons on the defensive and inhibits their ability to think and express themselves creatively.

8. *ENCOURAGE STUDENTS TO ASK THEIR OWN QUESTIONS.*

Questions are not just the property of the teacher, but can also be used effectively by the students.

9. *AVOID ECHOING STUDENT RESPONSE.*

There are two reasons for repeating student responses: to reinforce the answer or to state it loud enough so that others can hear who might have missed it the first time.

10. *ACCEPT STUDENT RESPONSES AS IF THEY WERE GIFTS.*

When a student ventures to answer a question he is risking something of himself. Every student hopes his answers will be accepted. Students will feel more confident to respond to open questions than to closed questions. Also, teachers will be more able to accept responses to open questions. We are not always perfectly pleased with every gift we receive, but we are usually gracious in receiving even the ones we are not pleased with.

PRACTICE LISTENING TO YOUR OWN QUESTIONS

With a tape recorder and a little time there are many ways that teachers can focus on their question asking skill and work at improving that skill. The first step is to record a portion of a class session where the teacher has planned to use questions to guide a discussion or to motivate further exploration. The next step could be any one of the following.

1. Write down all the questions you asked and categorize them according to the three categories of Information, Analytical and Personal.

2. Listen for how long a period of silence followed each question. Who broke the silence, the student or the teacher.

3. Listen for the kind of feedback you provide to students after they have made a statement.

4. Listen for the style of question asking: is it inquiry or interrogation?

5. Use a stop watch for a three to five minute period to measure how much time the students talk compared to how much time the teacher talked.

6. Listen for times when you could have followed up with a probing question, but did not. If you had thought to ask a probing question what would it have been?

CHAPTER TEN

CREATIVE USE OF MEDIA

We live in a day when persons are exposed to a wide variety of media in the home, school, community and church. In church education we can no longer depend upon the traditional teaching techniques which have been over-used by many teachers:

     **   just memorizing verses or facts,

     **   just listening to a teacher telling the lesson,

     **   just filling in the blank spaces in workbooks.

Students have become aware of multi-media, listening centers, individualized instruction, learning contracts, experiments, and many other features that are a part of the contemporary educational scene. It is imperative that teachers in the church seek creative, effective ways to motivate students to become actively involved in the process of their own learning.

There are some very basic presuppositions that underlie this chapter on **Creative Use of Media:**

1. *Teachers must assume responsibility for selecting or designing resources that are appropriate for their students.*

   The curriculum writer is writing for a national market. His suggested lesson plans can only be general and suggestive. Only the teacher knows the space available, the time available, the interests, needs and skills of the students, and his or her own resourcefulness. These factors must be considered carefully when planning a lesson or unit of study. Therefore, teachers must select resources and activities or must design some others that will be appropriate to the specific classroom.

2. *Some of the most effective resources and activities are the ones the teacher discovers or designs.*

   Many teachers have experienced the joy and excitement of planning an activity or using resources that were not specifically suggested in the formal curriculum. Teachers are more motivated when they invest their own creativity and students are more motivated because of the enthusiasm of the teacher and because the teacher has planned something for them.

3. *Students learn in many ways. A few learn well with verbal activities, many learn well with visual activities, but most students learn best when verbal and visual activities are combined.*

   Church education has traditionally focused upon written and spoken **words.** The students who could remember easily or who could verbalize well were the most reinforced and consequently the ones who participated most. The students who had less ability with words were often "turned off" to church classes. Teachers must realize that all students do not learn in the same ways; therefore it is necessary to provide a wide variety of learning activities so that all of the students will be reached in one way or another.

4. *Visual compositions are just as valid as verbal compositions.*

Because church education has focused primarily on written and spoken language we have forgotten the value of visual expressions to communicate meaning. In past centuries of the church's history there was a time when persons were unable to read the Scriptures in the native language. In order to communicate the truth of Scripture many visual means were employed: painting, mosaic, sculpture, tapestry, stained glass, and drama. Today it is possible that many students can be communicated with and can themselves communicate with these same media as well as films, filmstrips, slides, photographs, and other visual means. A visual statement by a student using a series of Write-On slides is just as valid as a verbal statement by another student.

5. *Audio-visual materials and equipment are not just tools for the teacher. They are also tools for the students.*

Most persons think of audio-visual aids as aids for the teacher. Today students are more and more able to use a wide variety of media to communicate with others as a response to some specific input or as a free creative expression of meaning.

6. *There are risks involved in using media equipment and resources, but the risks are worth it.*

Anyone who has ever used a film, filmstrip, or recording has had the experience of a bulb blowing, the film jamming, the adapter plug missing, or some other such calamity. I once conducted a workshop for sixty teachers on the creative use of filmstrips. After a brief introduction I pulled the screen down (it was attached to the ceiling) and it came loose from its mounting and hit me square on the head. After recovering quickly the only thing I could think to say was, "That's the risk you take in using media." Then next I said, "What is the alternative?" The alternative is to avoid using media, to show up with notes in your pocket or book in hand and **tell the students** what is important for them to learn. As far as I am concerned that is not a viable alternative. We must take the risk, even getting hit on the head, in order to use these dynamic resources in order to involve the students more actively in their own learning.

7. *Teachers and students must experiment and practice with media in order to use it creatively and effectively.*

Many times teachers try to use media equipment or resources without first practicing, previewing, or testing in order to feel comfortable and confident with their use in the classroom. If the equipment or resources do not work the way we hoped they would it may be because we have not worked with them enough to know what to expect. The same is true when encouraging students to use or create with media. They need the opportunity to practice and experiment in order to know how to use it to express themselves or communicate with others.

What follows is an outline of a variety of ways to use several media resources: filmstrips, slides, overhead projector, cassette recorder, and 16mm projector.

In conducting a workshop that emphasizes media it would be best to select just one or two media as the focus for the workshop. Teachers will be helped most if they can experience directly demonstrations of the media methods that are introduced and then have a chance to practice with the media. The suggestions listed below are just a beginning. You will know of and discover many more creative uses of media.

WAYS TO USE THE OVERHEAD PROJECTOR

1. **Instead of a blackboard.**

   If for no other reason this would be reason enough to purchase and use an O-H projector. Teacher is able to maintain continual visual contact with the students. Also, materials written on transparencies or acetate roll can be recalled quickly for review or emphasis.

2. **Teacher prepared materials.**

   Teachers are able to prepare charts, maps, assignments, outlines, etc., in advance of the class period to have available at the required time. Materials can be original, traced from book or copied from another source.

3. **Student reports.**

   In small groups or individually, students can prepare reports, outlines or other material to share with the whole class. By use of the overlay technique more than one report can be presented at a time if each group had prepared its material on a different section of the transparencies.

4. **Student creativity.**

   Students use many media to express their creativity. The overhead projector suggests many ways for the students to express themselves:

   1. illustrated story,
   2. a "movie roll" by using an acetate roll,
   3. opaque collage,
   4. opaque puppets.

5. **Map study.**

   The overhead projector lends itself very well to map study. By tracing a map from an Atlas teachers can give blank map to students for their marking of boundaries, routes, cities, etc. The use of overlays makes it possible to present several items on one map, possibly by different groups of individuals preparing separate materials.

6. **Opaque puppets.**

   Puppets can be created by using cardboard to cut out profiles of faces or silhouettes of persons or objects. By attaching the jaw of a face with a paper fastener it is possible to simulate talking.

7. **Opaque collage.**

   Many opaque materials lend themselves to creating a collage for the overhead projector: buttons, string, rubberbands, pipe cleaners, popcicle sticks, toothpicks, yarn, etc. Students can create very beautiful and expressive collages to convey a wide variety of feelings, meanings, or images.

8. **Picture lifts from magazines.**

    Picture lifts can be used to illustrate words to songs, or Scripture, to express feelings or impressions, or to create particular designs. This process can be employed by the teacher for his own purposes or be used by the students to involve them in the process of their own learning and creativity.

9. **Scenes with transparent and opaque figures.**

    By use of opaque silhouette cut-outs and transparent overlays with a color cellophane background it is possible to prepare an illustrated story adding an item at a time. The effect is similar to use of flannel board.

10. **Projecting words of songs, Scripture, etc.**

    It is often helpful to project the words of songs that people are not familiar with so that they can sing more confidently. Also, many recorded songs that are unfamiliar can be appreciated and understood better if the words are projected. The same is true for Scripture and other types of readings.

11. **Enlarging materials.**

    Maps, charts, illustrations, etc., can be enlarged by first tracing original material on a transparency and then projecting on a chalk board, newsprint, poster board, cloth, or some other materials which can be cut out, mounted, or displayed in permanent place. Use felt pens, crayons, a piece of chalk to trace around projected image on the particular material.

WAYS TO USE FILMSTRIPS

1. Present information to introduce a concept or an event.

   Show the whole filmstrip or just part of it.

   The filmstrip could be shown to the whole class or individuals or small groups could see it in a learning center.

2. Teacher can use the filmstrip and write his own script. This would be done for several reasons:

   — the script was intended for a different age group.

   — the script was inadequate, out of date or too long.

   — the teacher has particular objectives to accomplish.

3. Students can work in a small group to select frames for which they would write their own script. This could be done even if they have not previously seen the filmstrip and heard the script. The students could then record their script with a cassette recorder.

4. Students can view filmstrip without script and write captions for frames selected by the teacher. This is especially effective if the students identify with a character in the filmstrip and write their captions in the first-person. View the filmstrip a second time with students sharing their captions.

5. Show filmstrip to focus on specific characters so that students can identify with the persons in order to participate in a follow-up role-play activity.

6. Teacher and students can view the filmstrip without the script and discuss selected frames while they are being projected.

7. Stop filmstrip in the middle and discuss possible endings before showing the rest of the filmstrip.

8. Show filmstrip in order to set the stage and motivate students for a follow-up creative activity.

9. Project two filmstrips on the same subject simultaneously or project a filmstrip with another medium such as slides, 16mm film, or student created filmstrip.

10. Use Write-On filmstrip material for students to create their own visuals to accompany the script.

WAYS TO USE SLIDES

1. Give each student four or five Write-On slides to create his own story-line or message in response to the concept they have been discussing.

2. Students could work in small groups to create stories that include 15 to 20 frames.

3. Teachers could give students a script from a filmstrip they have seen and encourage students to create their own slides to accompany the script.

4. Using any of the slide formats (Write-On, picture lift, camera-produced), students could illustrate a song, poem, or passage of Scripture.

5. Teachers could use Write-On slides to present new words, visual illustrations of difficult concepts, symbols, stories, etc.

6. If two projectors and screens are available, camera produced slides could be projected on one screen and handmade slides projected on the other screen.

7. Given a page of twenty photo slides (camera produced) and two blank Write-On slides, students could select four photo slides that have something in common with each other or that communicate a message. Then use the Write-On slides as title slides to tie together the other four slides.

8. One key word, saying, sentence, or verse could be selected as the primary focus. Each person then creates one slide (from any format) to express the meaning of that statement as he "sees" it. All of the slides of the group are then shown without comment to express the variety of meanings of the single concept.

9. Write-On slides or scratched slides lend themselves to illustrating familiar symbols or designing new ones.

10. Try creating a litany with slides instead of just verbal statements. Each student could create his own visual statement. When all slides are collected, teacher or class can decide on a verbal response. Then project slides one at a time with the whole group responding verbally after each slide.

11. Because of the transparent element of Write-On slides, they can be placed over cartoons, line drawings, or other simple designs in order to trace the figure on the slide.

12. Each person could create his own slide or slides which tell something special about himself. Then as slides are projected, each person can introduce himself by interpreting his slide.

13. For prayer, have persons write or symbolize a problem, need, or person as a focus for prayer. With projector and slides it is possible to have a silent, visual prayer. Try this with appropriate background music.

14. Make slides of pictures in magazines to use as illustrations to accompany phrases of a song, poem, story, passage of Scripture or other materials.

COMMENT: When students select or create slides to illustrate particular images or concepts in songs, poems, or Scripture they not only facilitate the visual expressions of the material, they also accomplish several other things. By using contemporary visual images there is an "updating" of material, such as Scripture, which makes the images as relevant and new as last week's magazine. Also, there is an internalizing of the meaning of the particular material. When illustrating the song "Sounds of Silence" one girl said, "I will never forget that song!" That is quite possibly a fact. Another factor is that students are using medium that really speaks to them. They have been bombarded with visual images all their lives through television. Through slides they are able to use the visual medium themselves to express meaning as they feel it and to communicate that meaning to others. Slides speak much more dramatically than the crayons, paste, paper, and glue we are accustomed to using in many of our school and church classrooms. Students of all ages and abilities can use slides very effectively.

15. Select and place at random 80 to 100 slides in a tray, then project and advance them in time to the music or other recorded material. It is surprising how often a series of provocative slides applies to any given material without prearranging the order of the slides. Use the same process with two projectors and screens for double the effect.

16. Students can pose a scene, design posters or sets, and photograph them to tell their own story of any historical event or Biblical happening they may choose. By writing, then recording their own script, students can create a very significant slide set to share with other classes, parents, or other groups.

COMMENT: It is true that most schools and churches do not have cameras that can be made available to classes. However, in most classes there will be a child with a parent who has the proper equipment and enjoys taking pictures. By recruiting such a parent for a series of class sessions and with proper orientation as to the objectives of particular projects, it would be possible to not only accomplish a very helpful project, but also to involve a parent in a significant way in the classroom.

17. There are many more possibilities for using slides in the classroom to be discovered by you and your students. Have fun!!

WAYS TO USE CASSETTE TAPES AND RECORDERS

— — The word "cassette" comes from a French word meaning "case." In this instance we are speaking of small, plastic cases for tape recordings. A cassette tape and recorder is the ideal way to incorporate the use of recorded resources and activities in the classroom.

— — Bob Bolt of Baltimore says: "Cassette recorders and tapes are the teacher's

— personal, pocket-sized radio station,

— personal, portable university classroom,

— audio magazine or journal,

— personal recording studio."

— — The use of cassette tapes can be classified in the following categories . . .

. . . Teacher prepared tapes for instructional use.

. . . Student prepared tapes for response and expression.

. . . Data collecting of student participation.

. . . Evaluation of classroom activities.

. . . Commercially prepared tapes.

— — Recently a group of six teachers spent thirty minutes brainstorming all the possible ways they could imagine for using a taperecorder in the classroom. They came up with fifty-nine different applications. Some of these are included here.

— — **Teacher prepared tapes for instructional use.**

1, One teacher can divide a class into smaller groups by putting directions and other items on a tape and encouraging a group of three to six students to work independently, with the tape recorder serving as the "facilitator" of the learning activities.

Pre-recorded instructions for a specific sequence of learning activities. Paper, pencils, worksheets, books, photographs, or other materials could be provided and incorporated into the activity. When giving instructions verbally, repeat them and then allow time for everyone to do what is expected. (Be sure at least one student knows how to operate the tape recorder.)

Pre-recorded stories without endings, or situations unresolved, which require students to listen, think, discuss, and respond in some way. By using a few young friends in your neighborhood you could dramatize the stories of situations with a variety of young voices.

Pre-recorded field trip for a small group of students with a parent or teenager helper. A tour of church facilities, the sanctuary, the library, a cemetary, a museum or other place could be conducted by the teacher and "expert" ahead of time, recorded on tape and then used by the students as a regular part of their class or as a special activity. This could be supplemented with photographs.

2. Many times teachers are unhappy with the printed or recorded scripts of filmstrips. It is possible to edit or rewrite the script, record it and have available a preferred script for use with the class.

3. Some teachers are not skilled in singing or playing a piano to guide student singing. A pianist could record some songs or the church choir could record some songs for the teacher to use in introducing music activities to the class.

4. The whole world is available to the classroom for the cost of a long-distance phone call and a $1.95 device that can be purchased from Radio Shack. The telephone pick-up device can be attached to the phone and connected to the recorder to record a phone conversation.

The teacher could call a missionary, churchman in public office, or other type of person who may have some significant input to offer to the class. As long as the person is told he is being recorded there are no legal problems.

— — Student prepared tapes.

1. Individuals or small groups of students can write scripts for already prepared filmstrips, or for their own handmade filmstrips or slide sets. After writing the script it could be recorded to accompany the visuals when presented to the rest of the class.

2. Some students who have difficulty writing stories, reports, or other written items may be helped if they are able to dictate them into a tape recorder.

3. For older students a recording of a class discussion could be used for evaluation by the whole class.

4. By recording conversations with students it would be possible to collect a variety of responses on a specific subject to use with parent groups or in teacher training.

5. Teacher could save a tape which was recorded early in the year to compare with another tape made towards the end of the year to see if any changes have occurred.

6. In teacher training persons often make assumptions of what represents typical characteristics of various age groups of students. By recording a number of conversations or interviews with individual students of a specific age group it would be possible to collect a variety of responses that would reflect the spectrum of typical concepts, thoughts, expressions, or interests of that age group.

— — Commercially prepared tapes.

There are many producers of cassette tapes in the religious and secular education field. Some are intended for classroom use while others are designed primarily for teacher education.

1. Many record stores have a wide selection of cassette tapes with recorded music. Recorded songs or instrumental music can be used in several ways:

    — As background music while students are arriving or perhaps during a creative activity period.

— To introduce a new song for students to learn to sing and then sing-a-long with recording.

— To illustrate with slides, photographs, or transparencies and present as a multi-media show.

— To focus a specific concept or concern and use as illustration, motivation for creativity, or inspiration for reflection.

2. The American Bible Society has produced a set of tapes that include recordings of the complete New Testament in Today's English Version. The recorded Scriptures can be used:

— as script for filmstrip or slide set,

— for small group listening,

— by teachers at home for leisure time listening.

3. The National Teacher Education Project has produced a starter set of cassette tapes to use in teacher support and education. These tapes can be used by individual teachers at home or by groups of teachers for a regular planning or training session.

4. Abingdon Audio Graphics features Dennis Benson with two series of cassette tapes. RAP and SOS (Switched On Scripture) are designed to be used in programming of youth classes and activities.

WAYS OF USING 16mm FILMS

— —   It seems to me that teachers often use films for the wrong reasons.

Films have been used in church education for years, but often they are used ineffectively or for the wrong reasons. Even though we would rather not admit our mistakes all of us can recall times when we have done the following:

** Seen a good film and decided to show it to our class regardless of its appropriateness.

** Decided to use a film as a time-filler because there was not enough else planned for that session.

** Thought the class needed a change of pace with a little entertainment.

** Ordered films from media catalogues without previewing them personally.

It is this use of films that often turns persons off to the value of films in teaching. Films in educational settings are not intended to be just projected lectures, time-fillers, or entertainment.

The medium of film has tremendous potential for achieving many educational objectives a teacher may have. Films can be used to **provide documentation** for a specific subject, to **motivate** persons to think, feel, or express themselves; to **introduce** a particular question, issue, or topic; and to **accompany** another, independent medium.

Ordinarily short films (5-15 minutes) are the most useful when teachers are confronted with limited class time of an hour or less. Short films are inexpensive to rent and can be shown more than once. Good, short films, such as the ones mentioned in a following section, can be used in several ways with the same group without becoming boring.

Creative teachers have discovered many, many ways to use films effectively in their teaching strategies. Following are several ways that have proven themselves by many teachers:

1. **View with a purpose.**

Before showing the film the teacher can state one or more questions for the students to think about while viewing the film. If several questions are stated the class could be divided into several groups, or students could make a choice of which question to focus on. After seeing the film the students could discuss questions in small groups or as a whole class. Other tasks could be assigned prior to the film such as looking for specific emphases or making a list in some specific categories. The value of this approach is that persons are much more actively involved in viewing if they have something specific to guide them.

2. **Show contrasting films.**

When using films to introduce a subject or to motivate persons to express themselves creatively there is real value in showing two short films related to the same subject. The films should have different points of view, different cinemagraphic styles or other contrasting characteristics that will provide a basis for comparison and discussion. Usually the two films would be projected separately, but there may be value with some films to project them a second time simultaneously using only one soundtrack or perhaps even a separate recorded song or spoken word.

3. **Show a segment of a film.**

There are no written or unwritten rules that require a person to show the entire film. Some longer films have very valuable, complete-in-themselves, segments that could be used separately. This would be more true of training or documentary types of films than of dramatic films.

4. **Show the film in the middle.**

Many films that are presenting a narrative or documentation of a theme or event can be stopped at one or more appropriate places in the midst of showing the film. At that point the teacher could:

— engage the class in a review and discussion of what they have seen to that point.

— involve the class in discussing what they anticipate might happen and why.

— leave the lights dimmed and encourage the students to reflect on the feelings of a particular character by speaking in the role of that character, in the first-person singular.

— lead the students to compare two or more sections of the film as additional information or experience is presented.

5. **Show a film with another media.**

Persons are very capable of focusing upon more than one media at a time. Use a film without soundtrack and play phonograph record or tape recording as the soundtrack. Films and slides can be projected side by side on the same screen or two screens. Films can be projected on mirrors, ceilings, weather balloons, and walls for added effect.

6. **Films and role-playing.**

Films which present situations involving persons with real concerns can be used to motivate the viewers to identify with those same concerns. **Before** viewing the film persons can be introduced to the character with which they are to identify. **During** the film the viewer focuses on the experiences and feelings of that person. **After** the film discuss the issues in the first-person from the perspective of the character who was selected. If several characters were selected, then it is possible to mix up the characters in small groups.

FOCUS ON CRITERIA FOR SELECTING AND USING MEDIA

The leader could make a presentation if time is limited or he could guide a discussion if sufficient time were available that might include some of the following points.

With many types of media available, from magazine photos to video-tape equipment, and with the large quantity of resources within each type of media it is important that church educators begin to develop a set of criteria that they can use to determine the value and usefulness of various media. It is not enough to judge material solely on the basis of personal preference or taste or even on the recommendation of someone else. The following list of statements and questions is not intended to be comprehensive, but rather suggestive of some important areas of consideration.

1. Does the resource open up a subject by presenting basic information clearly, objectively, and interestingly?

2. Does the resource focus upon significant questions or issues, which persons must consider seriously?

3. Are there direct or indirect connections between the subject of the resource and the essence of the Christian Gospel?

4. Does the resource invite students to think, reflect, imagine and respond with all the creativity and insight of which they are capable?

5. Are the students encouraged to discuss, explore, research, or act further?

6. Can the resource be used in more than one way or for more than one application?

7. Are there guidelines or other resources which will help the teacher use the material to best advantage?

8. Is the resource appropriate to the age group for which it is intended?

9. If the resource is new, then time should be provided to preview or experiment.

10. The resource should not be so familiar that the students will be bored in its use.

11. The resource should not be so novel that it calls attention to itself causing its value to be lost.

12. The resource should be enjoyable and provide for the students a sense of satisfaction or accomplishment in its use.

By applying these criteria to a specific media resource it should be possible to determine whether or not the item is worth using or buying. If a resource receives a negative response to several of these criteria, then perhaps its purchase or use should be reconsidered.

CHAPTER ELEVEN

VALUES AND TEACHING IN CHURCH EDUCATION

Educators, pastors, parents and others in the Church have been concerned for centuries with teaching Christian values. Much preaching and teaching in the Church has focused upon the importance of adopting and living by values that are consistent with the life style and teachings of the prophets in the Old Testament and with the life style and teachings of Jesus Christ and the apostles in the New Testament.

In the Parable of the Two House Builders, Jesus said, "Those who hear my words and **do** them are like the wise man who built his house upon the rock." Again in Matthew's Gospel, Jesus said, "As you **did** it to one of the least of my brethren, you **did** it to me." The emphasis in each of these passages is upon **doing** what needs to be done to serve others, to put into action what one says he believes or thinks.

The Church in its education program has always been concerned to motivate persons to put into action their beliefs, to behave in a way consistent with the teachings of Jesus Christ. The problem is that in the Church we have too often **told** persons what they **should** do. We have tended to moralize by imposing what we think is good or right or of value upon those we would teach. When one person implies that he knows what is right for another person and insists that the other person act accordingly, he is moralizing and taking the responsibility for deciding and acting away from him. The moralizing process does not help a person to become responsible, mature, and independent in his choosing and behaving.

Dr. Sidney Simon and his colleagues have suggested an alternative to moralizing in forming values. The process they propose is identified as **values clarification.** This approach to forming values places a lot of trust upon the other person. The process says that there are many divergent, competitive, alternative values and that persons must choose for themselves how they are going to live their lives and be responsible for those choices. It does not mean that adult teachers or parents ignore the students, or leave them completely on their own to decide. Rather, adults provide a climate, a structure and way of interacting with students that helps them to experience the seven steps of value formation.

In recent years there has developed a particular approach to teaching values in public schools which has been closely identified with Sidney Simon and what he calls "values clarification." It is interesting to me that from the public education sector we in the Church are finding direction and support for our task of teaching values. In what follows, I have depended quite heavily upon the experience and writings of Sidney Simon and his colleagues, especially their two books VALUES AND TEACHING and VALUES CLARIFICATION. I have attempted to adapt what was originally designed for public school teachers and to apply the concepts and strategies to church education. After a brief statement of some basic presuppositions I will present a design for a six-hour workshop on **Values and Teaching in Church Education.**

Presuppositions

1. Most church teachers, pastors and parents have traditionally communicated values through an approach described as moralizing.

    To moralize on values for a young person is for an older person to imply by his behavior and statements, "I have lived long enough to have gained enough experience and wisdom to know what is right for you. Listen to me and do what I say and everything will be alright." This approach works in societies where there is a generally agreed upon consensus of what is "right," but in a society such as ours with so many divergent and competing values it is not easy to always know what is right for oneself let alone for someone else. When an adult is imposing his values upon a younger person it is not helping him to become an independent, responsible, mature decision-maker.

There is another problem associated with the moralizing approach and that revolves around what is called **hypocrisy.** Hypocrisy manifests itself when the adult says, "Do what I say, not what I do." Also, hypocrisy is evident when a younger person behaves according to his own set of values when he is not in the presence of or under the authority of the adult, even though he may have assented to the adult's values in his presence.

2. In the absence of a commonly accepted set of values, some adults take a laissez faire approach.

What the adult is saying to the younger person is, "Everything is all mixed up. I'm not sure what is right or wrong. Experience is the best teacher. You are on your own to find out and decide what is right for you. Good luck." This approach is not very helpful either. It provides no guidelines for youths as they search for what is of value.

3. Another influence on value formation is the "hero" or the "model" that a person admires.

Most youth and many adults have a variety of heroes that they admire in sports, politics, religion, movies, T.V., etc. Many values persons have are directly related to the values perceived in their heroes. The problem with this approach to value formation is that the hero sooner or later falls off his pedestal. The hero is fallible and is unable to fulfill all of the unrealistic expectations of the devotee.

4. Values Clarification is a very helpful alternative to the above three approaches to formation of values.

Values Clarification is an approach developed by Sidney Simon and his colleagues from the University of Massachusetts. There are several basic characteristics and principles associated with values clarification:

** The individual is primarily responsible for the choosing and acting out of his own values.

** Persons are helped when teachers, parents, and others are nonjudgemental in their response to the person's searching to clarify his own values.

** Teachers and parents are most helpful when they encourage the identification and evaluation of various alternative actions.

** Persons need opportunities to reflect on their own values, to hear other people's values, and to affirm their own values in the presence of others.

Seven Aspects of Value Formation

Definition: Values are those elements that show how a person has decided to use his life.

Process of Valuing: Unless something satisfies **all** seven of the aspects or criteria we do not call it a value.

1. **Choosing freely** —

   Values must be freely selected if they are to be really valued by the individual.

2. **Choosing from among alternatives** —

   Only when choice is possible with more than one alternative from which to choose, do we say a value can result.

3. **Choosing after thoughtful consideration of the consequences of each alternative** —

   A value can emerge only with thoughtful consideration of the range of alternatives and consequences in a choice.

4. **Prizing and cherishing** —

   Values flow from choices we are glad to make.

5. **Affirming** —

   We are willing to affirm publicly our values.

6. **Acting upon choices** —

   For a value to be present, life itself must be affected. Nothing can be a value that does not, in fact, give direction to actual living.

7. **Repeating** —

   Values tend to have a persistency, tend to make a pattern in a life.

Values and Value Indicators

According to the seven steps identified previously, many things that we have thought to be values are not really values but rather **value indicators**. Our values usually grow out of what are identified as value indicators. The following ten categories are important aspects of a person's life but ordinarily do not fulfill all seven steps, or criteria, of value formation.

1. Goals or purposes
2. Aspirations
3. Attitudes
4. Interests
5. Feelings
6. Beliefs, convictions, ideas
7. Opinions, points of view
8. Activities
9. Worries, problems, obstacles
10. Likes or dislikes, preferences

Value-Rich Areas of Life

All persons have some values. They may not be able to articulate what their values are, but if they are making choices between alternative actions they do have values. The values clarification approach is a way to help persons identify, clarify, formulate, and express their own personal values.

There are some areas in our lives that are especially significant, that require of us to formulate some values.

1. **Money** — how it is obtained, used, treated.

2. **Friendship** — how we relate to other persons.

3. **Love and sex** — how we deal with intimate, sexual relationships.

4. **Religion** — what we hold as our basic beliefs.

5. **Leisure** — how we spend our free time.

6. **Politics and social organization** — who we vote for, how agencies are organized, what laws they pass.

7. **Work** — choice of vocation, time, energy spent working, attitudes towards work.

8. **Family** — how one behaves in relationship with parents, siblings, children, etc.

9. **Maturity** — what each person strives for to be responsible, independent, grown-up.

10. **Character traits** — what persons are like, the ways they behave.

What follows is a series of values clarification strategies that could be used by the teacher in the church classroom. For additional strategies read books on Values listed in the Bibliography.

A. **Values Voting**

Voting is an action with which most students are familiar. Voting is fun and involves everyone. Voting requires persons to make choices. Voting can set the stage for a very fruitful discussion after persons have identified their positions (values) on a variety of issues. The teacher or the students could prepare the statements on which the class will vote. Each statement is prefaced by the phrase, "How many of you . . .?" The next word could be "think," "would," "feel," "enjoy," "are," "wish," or any one of dozens of other words that introduce the issue in a way that makes the choices personal and specific.

Some Values Voting samples . . . . .

— How many of you think that memorizing Bible verses is a good teaching activity for children?

— How many of you would prefer to teach on a day other than Sunday?

— How many of you feel that teaching in the church is a personally fulfilling experience?

— How many of you think that the Church helps persons form their values more than the Mass Media?

— How many of you are excited about the future potential of Christian education?

The above questions were related to the topic of teaching in the Church. There are many very fruitful topics that can be used for this strategy of voting, as well as all the other strategies. These topics include: money, time, religious beliefs, politics, work, leisure, family, interpersonal relations, sex, school, material, goods, ecology, and others.

In the voting strategy, persons cast their votes by raising their hands if they are in the affirmative, putting thumbs down if they are in the negative, and crossing their arms in front of them if they have no response. If they have very strong feelings, then they can wave their hands or thumbs vigorously.

B. **Value Clarifying Responses**

Values clarifying responses are very simple, natural and rousing verbal behaviors of teachers that can assist students to reflect on their values. These responses can be employed in any teaching situation where teachers and students are interacting with each other.

1. Was that your own choice?

2. Was it a free choice?

3. What other alternatives did you consider?

4. What are some other possibilities?

5. Where would that choice lead? What would some consequences be?

6. What do you have to assume for things to work out that way?

7. How do you feel? Are you pleased with that?

8. How important is that to you?

9. Are you willing to tell others about your choice?

10. Do others know that about you?

11. Would you really **do** that?

12. What actions would that lead you to?

13. Would you do the same thing over again?

14. Do you do that often?

Notice that the above list includes two questions for each of the seven steps in the process of value formation.

C. **The Value Clarifying Discussion**

Whereas the Value Sheet is primarily an individual activity, the Value Clarifying Discussion is a group activity. The teacher serves in the role of facilitator and enabler of discussion. There are no "right" and "wrong" answers. There are many points of view. Students need to be helped to hear each other and respect their differences.

Value clarifying discussion could be initiated by:

1. Questions from Scripture or other sources.

2. Photograph, art, poster, or other sources.

3. Scene from a play.

4. Short movie.

5. Tape recorded excerpt from radio or T.V. news, talk show, or other program.

6. Words of a song.

7. Magazine article.

8. Peanuts comic strip.

9. Newspaper editorial, letters to editor, Dear Abby

10. Advertisement for product or propaganda for political candidate.

Questions can be formed and a discussion developed that would help students to think about and express their own personal values.

D. **Rank Order**

Every day persons make choices that reflect priorities they have placed on things they buy, time they spend, persons they are with, and in many other ways. The priorities we establish consciously reflect the values we have. A **Rank Order** is a statement that introduces a situation or asks a question which is followed by three or four choices. Students are to rank the choices from highest to lowest priority. After ranking there can be time to compare and discuss the choices.

Sample Rank Orders —

1. If you had $10.00 you did not need for something else, would you:

    — — buy some clothes?
    — — buy some records?
    — — buy some books?

2. Which do you feel Jesus would consider the greatest sin?

    — — not forgiving a person who asked forgiveness?
    — — ignoring a person who needed help?
    — — ridiculing another person?

3. If you could spend a day with anyone now living, who would you choose?

    — —   the President of the United States?
    — —   a hero of the World Series?
    — —   a television star?

4. If you had time, money, and skill to help solve society's problems, which would you work on?

    — —   saving the environment?
    — —   reducing the birth rate?
    — —   improving the education system?

Practice creating your own Rank Orders

(Also involve students in creating Rank Orders.)

1. Create some on any subjects of personal interest.

2. Create some using Jesus and his teachings as the subject.

E. **Alternative Actions Search**

Many times persons act or behave one way and later after some reflection they wish that perhaps they had acted in another way. Usually there are several alternative actions that are possible in any given situation. Persons are helped when they can identify a variety of alternative actions that are possible, then select the one that is preferred.

"Alternative Action Search" is a strategy in which the teacher presents in written or spoken form a situation-story that is open-ended, with many possible alternative actions. The task of the students is to search for the action they would prefer to perform.

What follows is one example:

The Situation

"You have been sent by your mother to get a prescription filled at the drugstore. Your sister is very ill and needs the medicine right away. Your best friend sees you leaving on your bike and asks to go with you. You say okay. On the way you see a car hit a dog that was running across the street. The car keeps on going, but the dog is lying beside the road. The dog is bleeding, but still alive. What would you do?

Instructions

1. With two or three other persons — make a list of all the possible actions you and your friend could take in response to this situation.

2. By yourself — select which actions you think you would consider doing.

3. Which **one** of these actions would **you** do? Why?

4. Compare your choice with the other persons and discuss your reasons for your choice.

Teachers can create their own Alternative Action Search situations to focus on the concepts they seek to emphasize in a given class session.

F. **A Value Sheet**

A Value Sheet is something that teachers can prepare for students to work on individually or in small groups. A Value Sheet is a list of thought-provoking questions based upon a statement, story, question, issue, or event that causes persons to make choices that reflect on their values. What follows is a sample Value Sheet and a list of criteria to consider in designing Value Sheets.

Read the Parable of the Good Samaritan in Luke 10:25-37. **Think about**, then **write** or **discuss** responses to the following questions:

1. What do you think about the action of the Priest and the Levite?

2. The Samaritan was considered an enemy to the Hebrews. Why did he stop?

3. If you were the injured person, how would you feel about the Samaritan?

4. What are some examples from your own experience that are similar to this story Jesus told?

5. Jesus told the Parable in response to the question, "Who is my neighbor?" How would you answer that question?

6. Think of someone you know who needs a neighbor. How can you be a neighbor to that person?

Several criteria to consider when constructing Value Sheets:

—— Do the questions allow for free choice?

—— Does the teacher's judgement shine through the questions? If so, reword the questions so that they do nor moralize or imply obvious right answers.

—— Are the questions focused upon areas about which students have some very definite feelings?

—— Does the list of questions relate to some of the seven steps in the valuing process?

—— Is there at least one question that encourages the student to reflect on his own action?

—— Is the climate such that students feel free to make personal choices and will be accepted no matter what the choice?

G.   **A Simulation Game: Something of Value**

OBJECTIVES

At the end of the simulation game students will be able to:

1.   Identify their own personal most important values.

2.   Compare the priority of their personal values with the priorities of other persons.

3.   Develop a sense of identity with other persons of similar values.

SETTING

Something of Value can be played with 20 — 50 persons. Less than 20 persons will reduce the possibilities for interaction between individuals and small groups.

Room should be arranged with chairs in clusters of three or four chairs each. There should be sufficient space to allow for movement of all persons and for regrouping the chairs in other configurations of five to eight chairs per cluster.

MATERIALS

The only materials needed are five 3 x 5 inch cards, a sheet of blank paper and a pencil for each person.

PROCEDURE

STEP 1:   Each person takes a seat in a chair in one of the clusters of three chairs. Each person is instructed to list as many items as are valuable to him. Give examples of various kinds of items which may be of value: school, a special friend, an automobile, a favorite dress, truth, faith in God, baseball, T.V., family, etc.

STEP 2:   After making a list including as many items as can be thought of in two minutes, instruct each person to select five of the most important items and rank them in order of importance. Write one value on each card. Place number (or rank) of the value on the back of the card. (1 for top value, 5 for lowest). This should take approximately two to three minutes.

STEP 3:   When everyone has recorded his top five values and ranked them in order, then the three persons in each cluster exchange their sets of five cards. Each person reads the other's values and then ranks them according to his own order of priority placing the numbers on the back. In this process each person will have read and ranked two other person's values in addition to his own. Time: three to four minutes.

STEP 4: Each person receives back his own set of five cards marked on the back with the order of priority as others valued them. Time is provided for each group of three to discuss among themselves the similarities and differences among them and the reasons for ranking them in the order they did. Time: five to eight minutes.

STEP 5: After sufficient time of discussion persons are instructed to find other persons with similar highest values. Each person should focus on his top one or two values and through circulation among the participants find others who share his most important values. Groups should be formed with minimum of three and maximum of six or seven persons. When a group is formed they are instructed to arrange their chairs in a part of the room that will then become "their space" for the rest of the game.

STEP 6: Each newly formed group then follows the following instructions:

a. Decide on a name to identify the group's values.

b. Decide on a slogan or motto to symbolize the group's values.

c. Discuss why the group's values are most important and decide on what to tell the rest of the persons about the importance of their values and how to convince others to join them.

d. Select someone to speak for the group.

Time: Ten to twelve minutes.

STEP 7: Call the whole group to order and allow each group maximum of two minutes to make its presentation.

STEP 8: After the small group presentations, allow five to seven minutes for individuals to circulate among the others to "evangelize" the others seeking "converts" to their own group.

STEP 9: When persons have had a chance to "evangelize" others, call for the groups to reform. Spend just a minute calling attention to the way the groups now appear. (Often there is no change in group structures, or if there is change it may be only one or two persons who have shifted. Occasionally two groups decide to merge.)

REFLECTION AND DISCUSSION

No simulation game should be played if there is not sufficient time allowed for discussion and reflection after the experience. The purpose of a simulation is to provide a common experience for the whole group, related to aspects of their life experience, and to use the game as a basis for analyzing factors which determine personal and social values.

Some possible discussion questions:

1. How did you like the game? Any reactions?

2. Are the values you selected really **your** values?

3. How did you feel when someone else ranked your values differently then you did?

4. How did you participate in the group's process of deciding on name, slogan and spokesman?

5. Were you successful in convincing someone else to join your group and accept your group's values? Why? Why not?

6. What would you do differently if you were to play the game again?

7. If the groups did not change much, how come?

8. What parts of our personal and social life did this experience simulate?

LEADER'S ROLE

The leader should make the directions clear, brief, and direct. Give instructions one at a time. Better to allow less time than too much. Be aware of where the participants "are at" in accomplishing their tasks. Be available to restate or interpret the directions for anyone who asks questions.

The leader could enlist one or more persons to assist as observers. Observe what is happening. Make notes by writing direct quotes of what is heard or exact descriptions of what is seen.

Some things for **observers** to look for:

1. How do students make their decisions?

2. How much group loyalty is there?

3. Are some students easily led or influenced by others?

4. Do some students dominate?

5. Are there any examples of mature negotiations?

6. Is there any difference between the way persons act alone compared to the way they act in a group?

The **leader** could make a summary at the end of the experience which could include:

1. Persons do have different values. Not always a question of right or wrong but rather of what is appropriate for me.

2. Person's values are influenced by others.

3. Negotiating as equals is more satisfactory than giving in to someone else or dominating another.

4. Persons need more practice in communication.

5. Persons need more assurance that their values are worth keeping and building upon.

FOLLOW-UP ACTIVITIES

—— Some possible creative activities could include making posters, banners, collages or murals focusing on specific values.

—— A film, speaker, recording, or field trip, might be planned to gain additional insight and information related to specific values.

—— Groups could continue for several weeks working on a multi-media presentation to communicate to others in the congregation or community the meaning and significance of their chosen values.

—— The Scriptures could be searched and discussed focusing on specific values and comparing the message of Scriptures to the contemporary scene. Several appropriate Scriptures include:

1. Joshua 24:14-28 . . . "Choose this day whom you will serve."

2. Psalm 15 . . . "O Lord, who shall sojourn in thy tent?"

3. Micah 6 . . . "What does the Lord require of you?"

4. Matthew 5-7 . . . Sermon on the Mount, many appropriate passages.

5. Matthew 16:24-26 . . . "If any man would come after me . . ."

6. Mark 12:28-34 . . . "What commandment is greatest of all?"

7. Romans 12 . . . "Do not be conformed to this world . . ."

8. Galations 5:16-26 . . . "Let the Spirit direct your lives."

—— Listen to radio or T.V. commercials or read ads in a magazine to determine what values are being presented. How do these values influence our own personal values?

CHAPTER TWELVE

WAYS TO INCREASE STUDENT PARTICIPATION

Students will be more motivated to participate in classroom learning activities when they are enabled to make an investment in what is happening. Whenever a person has something at stake he is more interested in the outcome. Too often teachers are the only ones who have an investment and something at stake in the hour's church school session. Teachers need to develop ways to help students to make an investment in the session too.

One way to encourage the students to invest in their own learning is to provide as many ways as possible for them to make decisions about what and how they are going to study. When students are offered a variety of alternatives in the way of activities and resources from which they can choose what they want to do then they are likely to participate more enthusiastically.

There are many, many decisions students can make in an hour's class session. Some decisions are inconsequential and others are more significant, but all opportunities to make decisions contribute to the student's sense of investing in his own learning. Students who are able to make choices about what and how they will learn are more motivated than students who are told everything they will do.

Students make decisions when they . . .

1. **decide** where to sit.
2. **pick** which person(s) with whom to work.
3. **choose** which materials with which to create.
4. **decide** which resource books to use for research.
5. **interpret** passages of Scripture in their own way.
6. **choose** which Scripture passages to read.
7. **select** which version of the Bible they want to read.
8. **state** answers to questions in their own words.
9. **rank** items in their personal order of priority.
10. **state** their own questions in their own words.
11. **elect** which learning center or activity to work at.
12. **determine** which words best describe a subject.
13. **decide** for themselves which values are most important for them.
14. **resolve** how they will act in particular situations.
15. **settle** on one or more items from among many.
16. **judge** for themselves from among various alternatives.
17. **decide** upon a role with which to identify.
18. **test** for themselves the success of several possibilities.
19. **choose** what they want to communicate through their creativity.
20. (**state** your own examples of student choices.)

Following are more examples of strategies and activities that can be used to involve students in deciding what and how to learn.

1.   Writing a Learning Contract.

Some students have experiences in school of writing their own learning contracts with the teacher. In order to write a contract a student needs to know something of the subject matter to be studied and all the possible activities he can do to work on the subject. With this background he may be able to fill out a contract like this one.

LEARNING CONTRACT

I plan to study the following subject(s):

I will use the following learning centers:

   1.

   2.

   3.

   4.

   5.

I will share the results of my study by:

I will be finished by:

_____   _____
                            students name

_____
date   teachers name

---

2.   Selecting from Several Activities

The teacher may set the room up with several learning or activity centers. Each center would have the instructions visible and all the resources necessary to do the activity. After an introduction to the subject the students could be given a list of centers from which they could choose the one they want to work in. A sample list of activities related to the study of Amos is listed below. This list of activities was prepared for a large group of older students. If you have fewer students then you plan for fewer centers. A rule of thumb I follow is to plan for one center for each four or five students.

ACTIVITIES FOR EXPLORING AND CREATING ABOUT AMOS

Note: Select one activity. Meet with others who have selected the same activity. Follow the brief instructions, use the available resources and work for 30 minutes to complete your assignment.

GROUP ONE: Use Filmstrip and Create a Script

— Preview the filmstrip quickly.
— Look at filmstrip again. Discuss each frame to determine what is portrayed.
— Work on 5 or 6 frames at a time with each person writing a caption or description or dialogue for one frame.
— Or, as a group talk about the frames and have one person serve as secretary to write what is said.
— Some frames can be omitted if necessary.
— Prepare to present filmstrip and script to the whole class.

GROUP TWO: Use Script and Create a set of Slides.

— Read through the script quickly.
— Decide on which frames to illustrate.
— Use materials available to create write-on slides.
— Some slides can present title, captions, or dialogue as well as pictures.
— Prepare to present slides and script to the whole class.

GROUP THREE: Use Photo Slides to Create a Presentation

— Decide on the content of the presentation: Amos song, verses of scripture, a paraphrase of Amos, etc.
— Select slides to illustrate the chosen content.
— Use as many slides as desired.
— Prepare to present slides and content to the whole class.

GROUP FOUR: Create a Map Presentation Using Transparencies

— Use Golden Book Atlas and other books with pens, pencils and transparencies to prepare a visual presentation.
— Consider the following questions:
    ** What were the boundaries of the Northern and Southern Kingdom?
    ** Where did Amos live, work, prophesy?
    ** What were some of the key cities and places?
— Prepare to present transparencies to the whole class.

GROUP FIVE: Create a set of Posters or Banners

— Select a statement of judgment and a statement of hope from Amos' writing.
— Use magazines, poster paper, burlap, felt, scissors, glue, etc., to create two posters or two banners, one a statement of judgment, and the other a statement of hope.
— Prepare to share your posters or banners with the whole class.

GROUP SIX: Write Brief Articles to Create Two-Page Newspaper

- Consider the geographical, political, social and religious situation of Amos' day and write several brief articles in newspaper style. Use your imagination.
- Use a variety of styles: editorial, news, letters to the editor, cartoon, society, human interest, etc.
- Use ball point pens to write on spirit masters in order to duplicate the paper for the class.

GROUP SEVEN: Prepare for Prosecution and Defense of Amos

- Consider Amos: the times, his writing, etc.
- Prepare a list of charges against Amos.
- Half the group write an argument for the prosecution.
- Half the group write an argument for the defense.
- Prepare to present your arguments to the whole class.

3.   Using a Tic-Tac-Toe Form

For those students who prefer some structure and yet want to make choices we developed a format that we called Bible Study Tic-Tac-Toe. I see this form as a way to help guide students to receive some input on a subject and then explore and reflect in creative ways. We used this approach in a Vacation Church School class of second through sixth graders. Notice the diagonal tract that has bold borders. This track includes all "input" activities. There are eight other tracks from which the student can choose. Whichever track he chooses will include one of these "input" spaces. After doing that activity first the student then does the other two responding-creating activities. We found that this format for planning was very helpful to the students and they enjoyed it. I would not suggest that all students be expected to use this format every week. However, it does offer a good change of pace.

BEING FOLLOWERS OF JESUS TODAY

Student's name _____

This program has been completed _____

teacher

DECIDE ON WHICH THREE SPACES IN A ROW YOU WANT TO COMPLETE

START IN THE BOX WITH THE **BOLD BORDER**

TRUST WALK	SELECT SLIDES	OPEN ENDED SITUATIONS
Make arrangements with a teacher to take a trust walk with another student.	Use the Slides Notebook to select 6 slides that illustrate how people can be followers of Jesus today. Write a caption for each slide.	Select one of the open ended situations from the **Story Starter** box and do one of the suggested activities.
CREATIVE ACTIVITY	**JESUS FORGIVES**	**CHOOSE A SONG**
Choose one of the cards from the Creative Activity Center to get instructions for an activity. Express your own ideas about being a follower of Jesus today.	Use the Jesus Forgives worksheet in the Roles of Jesus Center.	Use a songbook to choose one or more songs that say something about being a follower of Jesus. Ask a teacher to play it for you on the piano.
CHOOSE A PARABLE	**PUZZLE SQUARE**	**PLAY A GAME**
Look at the list of parables in the Index of GOOD NEWS. Select one parable that you think helps persons to be followers of Jesus today.	Play the Puzzle Squares activity with 3 or 4 other persons.	Play the **Community Game** with three other persons.

4. Following instructions on Worksheets

Teachers could prepare one worksheet for all students to use or several worksheets from which they could choose. Whichever way there needs to be a lot of openness with alternative activities provided for. Following are two samples of worksheets.

THE APOSTLE PETER

Some **resources** to use:

1. GOOD NEWS FOR MODERN MAN
   — Look up Peter in the Index and read some of the references.

2. PEOPLE OF THE BIBLE
   — Look up Peter in the Index and read the pages that describe the experiences of Peter.

Some **questions** to answer:

1. What are some words that best describe Peter as a person?
2. What kind of relationship did Peter have with Jesus?
3. What was Peter's importance to the early church?
4. What are some of the important actions of Peter?

Some **activities** to do:

1. Write a letter of recommendation for Peter to be considered as a minister for your church.

   or

2. Create a series of Write-On slides to describe the Apostle Peter and some of his actions.

   or

3. Write out a list of ten to fifteen Bible verses that summarize the important aspects of Peter's life.

WHO WERE THE TWELVE DISCIPLES JESUS CHOSE?

Step One: Use either of the following two books:

BIBLE ENCYCLOPEDIA FOR CHILDREN
YOUNG READERS DICTIONARY OF THE BIBLE

Look up the word **Disciple** and read the definition.

Step Two: Complete the sentence in your own words —

"A disciple is _____

_____

_____ "

Step Three: Find at least one place in the New Testament where the Twelve disciples are listed.

Use Bible references in one of the books or index in GOOD NEWS FOR MODERN MAN to find a place where the disciples are listed.

Hint: Look under the word **Apostle** also.

The twelve disciples (apostles) were:

1.	7.
2.	8.
3.	9.
4.	10.
5.	11.
6.	12.

Step Four: To find out more about the disciples or to help you remember their names you can choose to do one of the following fun things.

a.   Finish a crossword puzzle
b.   Use the study-scope tube
c.   Play a game of cards — Disciple Rummy
d.   Use the Electric Board
e.   See a filmstrip

5. Values Clarification Strategies

All values clarification strategies (see Chapter Eleven) require that students make choices. When using Values Voting, Rank Order, Alternative Action Search or any one of several dozen other strategies the students will have a chance to invest themselves in the whole process.

6. Analyzing and Personalizing Questions

The two categories of questions presented in Chapter Nine which call upon students to analyze and personalize the subject matter are examples of ways students can become more involved through the kinds of questions teachers ask.

7. Creative Activities

Whenever students are provided with enough input to help them think about and explore a subject they will be able to respond creatively to express some of their insights and feelings. There are dozens and dozens of possible creative activities that will turn students on. It is important to always have a variety available which will include at least one writing, one drawing, one visualizing, one construction, and one dramatizing activity. When this variety is offered then every student will usually be able to find something that suits him.

8. Simulation Activities

Simulation games and other activities are all examples of requiring a high degree of student involvement as they make decisions in the process of identifying with persons, situations and events. There is a lot of interaction among students and a lot of decision making in simulation activities. Most simulation activities require the participation of the whole class.

When students do make decisions and do participate actively or express themselves creatively it is important that teachers encourage and reinforce the students non-verbally as well as verbally. Dr. Ned Flanders, developer of the Interaction Analysis System has said, "The most important moment in the classroom is the moment after the student has said or done something." The importance of the moment is in what the **teacher does** in response to what the student says or does. Everyone needs feedback from others. We need to know what others think of what we say and do.

Students who receive encouragement, praise, and other reinforcing responses from teachers are much more motivated to participate and do more.

We all have our favorite way to respond to students. Usually we use one or two phrases that are more like a mannerism than they are consciously chosen responses. Each of us needs to expand our repertoire of responses so when we do say "great" it sounds as if we really mean it and it is not a worn out response that the students hear all the time.

Consider the following list. How many do you use habitually? Which ones could you add to your repertoire with a little practice?

THIRTY WAYS TO SAY "GOOD FOR YOU!" OR "YOU'RE OKAY!"

1. That's great!
2. Good work!
3. Thank you very much.
4. Good idea!
5. That's a good point.
6. I like that.
7. Very interesting.
8. Terrific!
9. You're on the right track.
10. Marvelous!
11. Thank you for . . .
12. Excellent work.
13. Right on.
14. You've got the right idea.
15. Groovy!
16. Nice going.
17. That's neat.
18. That's unique.
19. Keep it up.
20. Exactly.
21. That's much better.
22. What neat work.
23. Wow!
24. Far out!
25. Beautiful!
26. That's a good start.
27. You make it look so easy.
28. That's an interesting way of looking at it.
29. You really did a good job!
30. Add your own . . . .

CHAPTER THIRTEEN

DESIGNING TEACHER EDUCATION EVENTS

This chapter is written especially for pastors, church educators and others who are responsible for recruiting, training, and providing support for church teachers. However, if you are a church teacher feel free to read further. In fact, you may find some ideas in this chapter that you would like to share with your pastor, Christian education committee, church educator or superintendent. If you find something that you like why not underline it and then pass it on to someone else to think about and work on.

A. Importance of Teacher Education

There was a time when I thought that if I could just find the **right** curriculum then most of our problems of teaching would be solved. However, the more I have looked at and worked with curriculum in the form of teachers' manuals and students' workbooks the more I have realized that I will never find the **right** curriculum. There are many good curricula on the market. But, even in the best I have noticed a weak unit here and a weaker lesson there. A whole curriculum from Kindergarten through adult is not consistently excellent according to any one person's evaluation. When two of us evaluate the same curriculum we will probably identify different weak and strong points. That is the nature of individual differences and the nature of curriculum. Even though I do not ever expect to find the perfect curriculum I am convinced that curriculum is very important for ninety-five percent of the teachers. Most teachers are not able or willing to start from scratch to write their own curriculum. So, we must select a curriculum that reflects our churchs' goals for Christian education and our expectations of teachers and students. But, after we have selected a curriculum our work has only just begun.

The **most important task** for every church is to **recruit teachers** who are motivated to teach. After recruiting teachers then they must be equipped to teach by receiving training and support that will enable them to become skillful, resourceful and effective teachers. Even though a curriculum is selected it is very important to equip teachers to be able to make curriculum decisions; to think, plan, and evaluate as if they were "curriculum writers." Teachers who can do this will breathe life and excitement into whatever curriculum the church has selected.

Persons are not necessarily "born to be teachers." Some may have more natural ability than others, but all persons who are motivated to teach can be trained; equipped to become more competent and confident as teachers. The success of any teaching staff or educational program in a church will be measured directly in terms of the quantity and quality of the training and support of teachers that is provided.

Every church, large or small, should develop a strategy for teacher education that will provide the necessary training and support for its own teachers. The previous twelve chapters have been one attempt to focus on some of the skills that teachers need in order to become more effective teachers. What follows in this chapter is an outline of some things to consider when developing a strategy for teacher education. In the Bibliography which follows there are many, many additional resources that could be considered when developing an overall strategy of teacher education.

B. Some Thoughts About Recruiting and Support of Teachers

Before training for church teachers makes any sense, there must obviously be teachers to train. Recruiting teachers is one of the most difficult and frustrating tasks in church education. The difficulty may be more a symptom of other problems rather than the central problem itself. If recruiting is a symptom of other problems, some of those problems may be:

1. Poor image of the role of teacher.

2. Low priority of education in the church.

3. Invisibility of the education program to most of the congregation.

4. Teachers' sense of isolation and neglect.

5. High ratio of students per teacher.

6. Irregular attendance by students and little parent support.

7. Inadequate rooms, equipment, and resources.

8. Lack of time to do adequate preparation.

9. Teachers experiencing little sense of satisfaction and accomplishment.

10. Lack of professional training and support of teachers.

To the extent that any of the above problems are present in a church it is likely that it will continue to be difficult to recruit persons to teach. At all levels of the church's life there needs to be increased commitment to and support of the church teacher.

There are a variety of actions by pastors, church educators, official boards, education committees and others that may help to resolve some of the problems and perhaps make the task of recruiting more manageable.

1. *Instead of filling empty "slots" recruit persons with specific skills for specific tasks.*

   Often persons are recruited at the point of their weakness. Very few persons feel capable of teaching biblical and theological content. However, many persons have particular interests or skills such as photography, art, music, drama, story telling, etc. Why not recruit persons at the point of their strengths, asking them to contribute their skills and share their interests with the students. In order to do this a committee or recruiter needs to inventory the interests and skills of members of the church.

2. *Instead of recruiting persons for unspecified periods of time, establish clear beginning and terminating times which may be as long as two or three years or as short as one unit of study or several months.*

   Every person prefers to know exactly how long he is expected to serve as a teacher. To expect everyone to teach for a year or two may eliminate some excellent teaching prospects. A person with photographic skills may be able to work with a team of teachers for a unit of study where his skills could be used in one Learning Center. Even persons who are able to serve for longer periods of time are helped when they know how long they are expected to teach.

3. *Instead of recruiting persons to teach by themselves, develop a system of team teaching or at least team planning.*

Low morale develops when persons feel trapped and isolated in a class. These feelings can be overcome when teachers are able to work with a team of one or more other teachers. Even in small classes of ten or fewer students, there are advantages to team teaching. Teachers are able to bring a wider variety of skills and interests when there are two or more in a class. Also, it is possible to miss an occasional Sunday without disrupting the continuity of the class. Even where it is not possible to recruit teams of teachers to teach together it may be possible to develop teams of persons who can **plan** together to assist the solo teacher in planning.

4. *Instead of placing persons on teaching teams like "blind dates," provide for a process for persons to work together in training sessions or other situations where they will have an opportunity to "court" each other to decide for themselves with whom they want to teach.*

Persons who are able to choose the person with whom they will teach will be more motivated to work on developing a team relationship than if they are just told which team they will be on. Often it is possible for persons to be encouraged to recruit their friends to teach with them. I think we are very unfair and unrealistic when we just assign persons to teach together without carefully assessing the potential problems or values of particular persons working together.

5. *Instead of approaching persons about teaching in general, a clear statement of expectations should be presented to the prospective teacher.*

Teachers will be able to evaluate themselves better if they know exactly what is expected of them. One church prepared the following list of expectations:

What Do We Expect of Teachers?

When a person accepts the challenge and the responsibility to teach in the church school the Division of Educational Ministry understands the following to be essential for the fulfillment of the purposes and goals of Christian teaching and learning:

a. Teachers see their task as a specific response to God and the Church expressing their Christian Commitment.

b. Teachers become members of teaching teams —
   - in relation to children of a particular grade, taught with other teachers
   - in working with other teachers — guidance will be provided by a lead teacher
   - a larger team representing the Children's Department will assist and guide the teachers in their work.

c. By participating with a Team of Teachers and through planning ahead there will be opportunity for occasional Sundays off.

d. Teachers continue to express themselves and find inspiration for their work through the corporate worship of the congregation.

e. To do their work well teachers must:

   — first complete a Teacher's Basic Training Course
   — participate with the teaching team in planning and preparation of weekly lessons
   — do systematic and careful planning for each class session
   — be regular and prompt in attendance where their participation is depended upon
   — attend regularly the planned Teacher Enrichment sessions sponsored by the Division of Educational Ministry.

f. The Church School year is from the First Sunday after school begins to the second Sunday of June. Teachers are expected to serve for the full year. Before the end of the year teachers will have the opportunity to meet personally with a member of the Recruiting and Training Committee for the purpose of reviewing and evaluating the year's work and for discussing the teacher's placement in the Church School the following year.

Another church prepared a little booklet entitled, "Me? A Teacher?"* which introduces the teaching ministry of the church. One section of the booklet describes the role of the teacher as follows —

"A TEACHER isn't a Bible expert, BUT — has professional help and guidance.

   Curriculum materials do not assume that teachers are Bible authorities. Resource materials provide thorough Bible background. Staff members are always ready to help.

"A TEACHER doesn't know all the answers, BUT — is a learner among Learners.

   The teaching process emphasizes the teacher as a guide — a fellow discoverer. The teacher is not embarrassed if he does not know the answer. He says, "Let's find out together."

"A TEACHER isn't tied to a rigid program, BUT — is free to be creative and flexible.

   The teacher can make use of his own special talents and avoid those areas which he finds difficult or awkward. The teacher may call upon resource persons for some parts of the program.

"A TEACHER doesn't teach a curriculum, BUT — teaches persons.

   The teacher attempts to meet the needs of each student. Students remember teachers long after the lessons the teachers teach. God works through persons to reveal his love and truth.

"A TEACHER doesn't teach all the time, BUT — takes time to listen.

   Maybe this is the only place the child can talk to an adult who listens and really cares.

*This material is quoted from a booklet prepared by Mrs. Donna Mason, Director of Christian Education at Fremont Presbyterian Church in Sacramento, California. Our thanks to Donna!

"A TEACHER doesn't do it alone, BUT — is part of a team.

> Life together in the church is team-work. Teaching in the church requires team-work between teachers and students, between teachers and other teachers, and between teachers and other staff."

6.   *Instead of expecting teachers to learn how to teach by teaching provide a regular program of pre-service and in-service training.*

There are many ways to provide training for teachers which are developed further in this chapter. However, consider the following:

   a.   Provide an annual "Introduction to Church Teaching" course to introduce the roles and skills of teaching. This course could be part of the regular adult education program and offered to parents, new members, older youth and others who are potential teachers.

   b.   Encourage persons to get acquainted with teaching by serving as teacher's aides for a short period of time.

   c.   Maintain an "open-door policy" which will encourage persons to feel free to visit church classes to observe teaching in action.

   d.   Publish a quarterly or annual list of all training opportunities that are available locally, regionally, denominationally or through public agencies.

7.   *Instead of recruiting teachers and leaving them on their own or forgetting about them, provide for a regular program of teacher recognition.*

Teachers will hardly ever ask to be recognized. They should not have to ask. Superintendents, committee members, church educators, pastors, and others can find many ways to provide recognition of the teaching staff. It is important to the whole church that the teaching ministry be very visible. Programs will never be established as high priority for budget or persons' commitments, unless they are visible and obviously worthwhile. Some ways to recognize teachers include:

   a.   Write-ups of teachers and/or class activities in weekly bulletin and/or monthly newsletter.

   b.   Listing of teachers with others of the official church boards.

   c.   An annual church school open house.

   d.   An annual reception for teachers.

   e.   A service of dedication for teaching staff.

   f.   Displays, exhibits and reports of student activities, projects, and creativity.

   g.   Sharing of student produced materials with other church groups or in congregational dinners or worship services.

h. Inviting representatives of the teaching staff to make brief informal reports to the official church board several times a year.

i. Occasional phone calls or personal visits to teachers by someone on the church staff or official board.

What is suggested above is just an outline of some possibilities for increasing the visibility, the importance, and the place of teaching in the church. The main point is that each church must develop a strategy that places teachers and teaching at the center of the church's concern for effective ministry. The challenge is for you to work with a few other concerned, responsible persons to review your present strategy and/or develop a more appropriate strategy.

C. Types of Teacher Education Events

Once a church has developed a strategy for the recruiting, recognition and support of teachers it is important to include in that strategy a systematic program of teacher education.

There are many types of teacher education events some of which are outlined below. Also, the first twelve chapters of this book could be used as guidelines for a program of teacher education.

What follows is a list of a wide variety of types of training events that are possible to offer for volunteer church teachers. These suggestions are not evaluated or placed in any particular hierarchy of value.

1. **Brief training period as part of regular teachers' meeting.**

   If teachers meet monthly or on some other regular basis it is possible to spend thirty to ninety minutes of that meeting on a specific resource, method, activity, skill, or concept related to the teaching task.

2. **Teacher briefing sessions for all teachers of one grade group.**

   When two or more teachers are using the same curriculum in one or more churches it is possible for them to meet once per unit to receive from each other or from a church educator a briefing related to the next unit of study.

3. **Self-instructional or guided training.**

   There are resources available in printed, recorded, or visual form that could be used by individual teachers or in small groups of two or three teachers. Teachers could participate regularly at their own convenience in a process of training and enrichment.

4. **The "one-night-stand" event.**

   One event of two or three hours scheduled for a group of teachers. These are the most difficult to conduct. There is little continuity between previous or succeeding events.

5. **The series approach.**

   Several events conducted weekly or monthly for a period of time. Each event is related to the others so that the whole series provides a systematic development of basic topics and skills.

6. **Intensive, developmental approach.**

Six or more events conducted in a relatively short period of time — two weekends, one week, or two nights each for three weeks. The basic components of the teaching learning process are identified, practiced, and evaluated.

7. **Small group, laboratory approach.**

A number of sessions with small groups of teachers representing similar age groups of students. Focus is upon specific needs of teachers as identified by leader and teachers. Work involves practice and observation of classroom teaching.

8. **Repeatable experiences.**

One or more sessions providing specific experiences that can be repeated in the classroom. Focus may be on content, teaching procedures, or use of equipment and resources.

9. **The "buddy system."**

Just about every church school teacher knows at least one public school teacher who teaches the same age group. Many professional teachers feel unable to teach on Sunday too. But, many of these same teachers would be more than willing to consult with a church school teacher on a regular basis. If a church school teacher were to seek out a professional teacher to be his or her "buddy" for a year a lot of good things could happen.

    ** The church school teacher could observe several times in the public school classroom.

    ** The two teachers could meet together occasionally for consultation and planning.

    ** The public school teacher could observe in the church school class and provide some helpful evaluation and critique.

10. **The community college or evening school course.**

In many communities the local school districts or colleges are offering courses designed for school professionals, nursery school teachers, scout and recreation leaders and others who serve in the role of leading or teaching in community programs. Some community colleges will offer courses on demand. That means, if a certain number of persons request a specific course and guarantee enrollment the course can be offered and tailored to those persons.

11. **Closed circuit or community television.**

The Archidiocese of San Francisco has its own closed circuit television station with receivers in all the parishes and schools of the diocese. Many communities are equipped with cable television, which by law requires that the station be responsive to community programming needs and interests. Such resources could be used to provide teacher education.

When one surveys a list such as outlined above it seems obvious that we should never feel ourselves limited by what is possible to offer to teachers. It is also very obvious that no one type of training event will ever meet the needs of even one teacher, let alone a whole teaching staff in one or more churches. Whoever is responsible for providing teacher education events for teachers must develop a strategy that will incorporate many approaches of teacher education and will encourage the teachers to be selective and respond to what they find of interest to them, of value in meeting their needs, and most convenient in terms of the time and location of the event. If church teachers are to become better equipped to teach, then a well-defined, promoted and implemented strategy must be developed that will reach the teachers where they are, in their local communities with specific needs and responsibilities.

D. Teacher Education for Churches Without Professional Staff

Most churches of all denominations can be classified as small to medium size in church membership and church school enrollment. For the purpose of this presentation I would identify all churches **under** 350 to 400 members in this category. Very few churches of this size have even part-time professional educational staff and fewer still have full-time staff. Yet, teachers in these churches need the support and guidance just as much as the teachers in larger churches who can afford educational staff persons. Teaching effectiveness in all churches is not going to improve unless more time, energy, money and commitment are invested in equipping teachers with insights, skills, resources, and motivation that will enable them to do a better job.

What follows is an outline of several strategies that could be considered by smaller churches in order to provide teacher education services to their teachers.

1. Several churches in one town of different denominations or several churches of one denomination in a geographical area could combine some personnel, some money, and some resources in order to:

   a. hire a part-time or full-time educational staff person;

   b. establish a teacher education committee to plan, promote and implement a teacher education program;

   c. develop a media resource center to pool all media resources and purchase new materials that could serve all the churches; and

   d. form a "leadership pool" by identifying and enlisting persons in the churches and community with special skills who could provide training or assistance to teachers in specific skills or subject areas.

2. A church could identify and enlist two or three persons from the church membership who have had experience with teaching and provide them with specialized training in order to serve as volunteer leaders of teacher education in their church. The Teaching Skills Institutes, sponsored by the National Teacher Education Project, are excellent programs to provide basic training for persons who would seek to lead teacher education programs. It is important that more than one person from a church participate in this type of program so that when they return to the church they can work together and be supportive of each other as they seek to provide leadership in their church.

3. The pastor of a smaller church who is interested and skillful in church education could enlist several persons to work with him to provide for teacher education in their parish. The pastor could provide teacher briefing on the subject matter for a unit of study and one

or two other persons could provide the briefing regarding teaching activities and resources for the same unit of study.

4. A teacher education coordinator or small committee could work on providing a "buddy" for each teacher on the staff. (See Section C, item 9)

5. A teacher education coordinator could borrow, rent, or purchase from a denominational office, resource center, or bookstore one or more of the packaged, self-instructional teacher education modules for use by teachers in a planned, coordinated way.

It should be apparent that any of the above could be used by itself, but that several of the strategies when used together in a coordinated way would provide for maximum effectiveness.

The primary implication is that someone, or several persons, in a church must become aware of the need for teacher education in their church and assume responsibility for implementing a helpful program. There needs to be an overall cooperative, coordinated strategy developed by each church. It is most desirable for several churches to work together.

E. Necessary Components to All Teacher Education Events

In conducting teacher education events throughout the country for groups of thirty to three hundred persons representing a wide spectrum of denominational affiliations, I have concluded for myself that the following methods work best.

1. Take the stance that "we are all in this together." No one is an expert. We are all teachers with more or less experience than the other, but each one of us wants to become more skillful in teaching. Keep the workshop low-key, so that persons are helped to feel comfortable about themselves, each other, and their tasks as teachers.

2. Keep lecture presentations to a minimum. In a three-hour workshop thirty to forty minutes of lecture would be the maximum.

3. Involve persons in experiencing teaching activities and resources. Use these direct experiences as frames of reference for identifying important educational principles.

4. Plan for teaching activities that persons can adapt and use in their own teaching situations.

5. Provide many opportunities for persons to interact with each other in small groups. Plan for small groups to report or share with the whole group the results of their discussion, research, or creativity.

6. Use a variety of media resources during the workshop.

7. Duplicate materials that can be distributed to persons to take home with them.

8. Provide several tables of display materials and resources for persons to browse and preview.

9. Use a large room for the workshop. Arrange the room with persons seated comfortably at tables.

10. Use an overhead projector as a means to provide visual communication by using prepared trans-

parencies, displaying small group reports, recording responses by participants, or illustrating key concepts.

11. Plan the training event in such a way that the process used for the event will teach, in addition to the content of the event.

12. Respond to persons after they have said or done something in such a way that they receive positive reinforcement.

13. Encourage persons to express themselves freely and creatively by being open to and receiving what they offer.

14. Everything that is done and said in the workshop should be very practical so that the experienced teacher can build on what is offered and the inexperienced teacher can be helped to implement what is offered.

Just as teaching is an art, so is designing and leading teacher education events. Many persons have attended a lot of training events from which they have received very little practical help. After attending a teacher education event, all the participants have the right to expect that they will be helped to be able to do something different the next week in their classroom. Those who lead teacher education events need to set high standards for themselves so that careful preparation will be made and helpful leadership will be provided for every event. Too many teachers have already been exposed to too many poorly-planned, and sloopily-presented workshops. Let's not add any more of these.

F.   Ten Descriptions of Teacher Education Events

The following descriptions represent what I believe to be some of the more important subjects for teacher education events. Subject matter and resources for most of these ten events are included in the first twelve chapters of this book. Each of these events could be conducted in a minimum of three hours. However, it is possible to take parts of each event for a shorter period of time or to expand each event for three or more additional hours. It is assumed that each event could be led by one person, however, it would be very possible for a team of two or three leaders to conduct each event. What is presented in each description is what I include in the training events I conduct by these same titles. You will want to add, subtract, and adapt the descriptions to fit your situation and to represent your highest concerns. There are many ways to design each event to achieve the objectives as they are stated.

1.   **PLANNING FOR TEACHING**

(A 3 hour workshop for teachers)

Teachers usually depend upon a given curriculum for determining the overall content of their teaching. However, curriculum writers write for a national market that may or may not be similar to the teacher's own situation. Most teacher's manuals offer much more to teach than is possible. Therefore teachers need help to decide what to teach in the given situation. Learning experiences for students of all ages need to be planned creatively in order to motivate and involve students in the process of their own study and discovery. This workshop will focus upon some very specific, helpful steps that teachers can take to plan for creative teaching.

Through this workshop teachers will be enabled to:

1.   Identify key concepts for teaching and be selective of what to teach in a limited time.

2.   Determine specific instructional objectives that will guide teacher planning and student activity.

3.   Select teaching activities and resources to communicate the key concepts and achieve the objectives.

4.   Use several helpful criteria to evaluate their teaching plans.

5.   Use a specific process for lesson planning in relation to their own curriculum.

6.   Practice planning for teaching using **The Planning Game.**

2.   **TEAM TEACHING IN CHURCH EDUCATION**

(A 3 hour workshop)

One feature of Christian community is that persons share together responsibility for the whole ministry and mission of the church. In church education there are many very positive values to team teaching that provide support for the teachers as well as enhance the learning of students. Especially with new emphasis on open classrooms, individualized instruction, and multi-age learning groups it is important to equip teachers to serve effectively on teaching teams.

In this workshop participants will:

1.   Develop a workable definition of team teaching that can be implemented in their own situations.

2.   Experience several examples of team planning and decision making.

3.   Review several alternative models of team planning and teaching.

4.   Discuss their own needs and desires regarding their role as teachers.

5.   Consider a checklist of ten steps toward effective team planning and teaching.

Resources used in this workshop will include a filmstrip: **The Group Way of Teaching** and one or two simulation games: **Teacher Survival, Teaching Strategy,** or **The Planning Game.**

3.   **GOD THROUGH THE EYES OF A CHILD**

(a 3 hour workshop)

Teachers and parents are more effective when they are able to understand God, Jesus, Church, Bible, and the world from the frame of reference of those whom they teach. Children start with primitive concepts and grow in their understanding of God. They are not able to comprehend adult concepts. Therefore, adults must work extra hard to look at abstract concepts through the eyes of children.

Participants in this workshop will:

1.   Hear a brief presentation on the conceptual development of children.

2.   Explore ways children grow in their thinking about God.

3.   Identify some of the difficult questions that children ask of their parents and teachers.

4.   Preview a variety of resources that can be used in teaching children at church and home.

5.   Experience some ways children have expressed themselves about God, Jesus, Church, and Bible through creative writing and art.

4.   **INCREASING TEACHER-STUDENT INTERACTION**

(A 5-6 hour workshop)

Much teaching in the church relies upon the spoken words of teachers and students. Most observers of church teaching report that teachers do 75-90 percent of the talking that occurs in the classroom. It is true that students are most motivated to learn when they are actively involved in their own learning. There are many ways teachers can increase student involvement through verbal activities. This workshop will enable participants to:

1.   Identify Flander's ten categories of teacher-student talk and to use the process of Verbal Interaction Analysis as a tool for evaluation of classroom talk.

2.   Employ several basic rules in developing verbal and written instructions for classroom activities.

3.   Identify three general categories of questions and to prepare questions in each category.

4.   Develop a checklist of a dozen principles to follow when engaging students in interaction.

5.   Work with other teachers in a process of mutual support and critique to improve their skills of direction giving, reinforcement, and question asking.

Several taped, filmed, and programmed resources and activities will be used to involve participants directly in working on the skills necessary to achieve the above objectives.

5.   **CREATIVE WAYS TO STUDY AND TEACH THE BIBLE**

(A 3-10 hour workshop)

The Bible is the basic textbook of church education in teaching children, youth, and adults. All persons would be helped to read, study, and interpret the Bible so that its message becomes relevant to their own lives. It is not enough to just read a few verses and discuss them, or to memorize a few selected verses, nor to fill in the blanks of a workbook. Creative studying and teaching of the Bible requires that persons develop a few basic skills and have available some basic resources. The most effective way to learn is to be involved directly in the process of exploring scripture and applying its message to contemporary situations.

As a result of participating in this workshop persons will be enabled to:

1.   Use several basic skills and resources for their own study of the Bible. (Resources to include: Concordance, footnotes, Dictionary, Commentary and Atlas.)

2.   Compare inductive and deductive teaching styles.

3.   Identify several basic principles that apply to the teaching of scripture with any age group.

4.   Repeat several of the six to ten different experiences of Bible study in their own classroom.

5.   State the value of using a variety of media resources in teaching scripture.

6.   Decide which resources will be needed for teaching the Bible in their own Classroom.

The approaches to teaching the Bible experienced in this workshop are of the same style and approaches as the ones included in the book TWENTY NEW WAYS OF TEACHING THE BIBLE.

6.   TRANSLATING THE BIBLE THROUGH TEACHING ACTIVITIES

(A 6-9 hour workshop)

One of the primary activities of the Christian Church has been the translation of the Holy Scriptures into the languages of the people of every land. In our land, in this day one of the important areas for translating scripture is in the church classroom. Students of all ages need to hear, read, and experience the Scriptures in a "language" they can understand and respond to. In many ways the church teacher serves as a translator. In order to become effective translators teachers need to develop skills, use resources, and devise strategies that communicate the Good News. This workshop will involve participants with a wide variety of teaching activities that can be repeated or adapted for use in their own classrooms.

In this workshop participants will:

1.   Consider the role of translator as a primary role for the church teachers.

2.   Review ten important decisions every teacher must make in the process of planning and teaching each lesson.

3.   Be involved in a series of creative teaching activities focusing on Old and New Testament.

4.   Experience directly two brief simulated activities as models for teaching the Bible.

5.   Explore a variety of resources that are available for creative teaching.

This workshop is designed especially for teachers grade three through adult classes. Teachers of younger children will find helpful insights for their own personal Bible Study and will be able to apply many of the basic principles to their own teaching.

7. **CREATIVE USES OF MEDIA**

(A 3-6 hour workshop for teachers)

Persons live today in a world of media. Homes, schools, churches and other institutions experience the influence of a wide variety of media. Persons can communicate more effectively and learn more when they are enabled to use all of their senses in the process. Teachers have access to much media already and can with little effort procure or devise many other media resources. This workshop will focus on ways teachers can use media to prepare their own lessons as well as ways to involve students in the use of the same media.

In this workshop teachers will be enabled to:

1. Use several media resources and equipment.

2. Express in a creative form several key concepts that are related to a future lesson plan.

3. Identify the criteria for selecting and using media.

4. Select several items to recommend for future purchase and use by their church.

5. Recall a dozen or more ways of using several media.

Two or more of the following resources may be selected as the focus for the workshop. Slides without a camera, slides with a camera, cassette tape recordings, Overhead projection, filmstrips, 16mm films, teaching pictures and study prints, or phonograph records.

8. **WAYS TO INVOLVE STUDENTS IN LEARNING**

(A 6 hour workshop)

Persons learn most effectively when they are involved in the process of their own learning. There are several keys to student involvement in learning activities: motivation, relevance to life experience, variety of teaching activities, and teacher's role in the classroom. Teachers make many crucial decisions in the process of their planning and while engaged in teaching that influence student involvement. Teachers can be helped to identify these moments of decision and to increase their skillfulness in making helpful decisions.

In this workshop participants will:

1. Identify several crucial classroom decisions that influence the level of student involvement.

2. Employ several basic rules in developing verbal and written instructions for classroom activities.

3. Compare inductive and deductive teaching style.

4. Identify three general categories of questions and to prepare questions in each category.

5. Develop a checklist of a dozen techniques to use when engaging students in their own learning.

6. Experience a variety of ways to approach the teaching of scripture.

7. Work with other teachers in a process of mutual support and critique to improve their skills of direction giving, question asking, decision making and reinforcement.

9.   **TEACHING VALUES IN CHURCH EDUCATION**

(A 3-6 hour workshop)

Education in the church has always been concerned about helping students to form Christian values. Traditionally the approach to value formation has been moralizing. There is another, more effective approach developed by Sidney Simon known as values clarification. This approach involves persons directly in the process of clarifying and forming their own values. There are dozens of specific strategies that teachers can use with students which increases their motivation, involvement and learning.

In this workshop participants will:

1.   Compare the differences between the moralizing and clarifying approaches to values formation.

2.   Identify the seven steps which result in the formation of a person's values.

3.   Experience six to ten different values clarifying strategies that can be used with students.

4.   Work on designing their own strategies for values clarification to present to the whole group.

5.   Discuss ways to implement values clarification strategies in their regular teaching situations.

A film VALUES SYSTEMS TECHNIQUES, featuring Dr. Sidney Simon, will be used in the workshop. The approach of the workshop will attempt to relate values clarification to biblical and theological concepts. This workshop is appropriate to teachers of all age groups and most especially youth.

10. INDIVIDUALIZING INSTRUCTION THROUGH LEARNING CENTERS

(A 3-10 hour workshop)

The Open Classroom, Contract Learning, Individualized Instruction and Learning Centers are approaches to teaching that are gaining wider acceptance in public education. The focus of these approaches is to design learning activities appropriate to the skills, interests, and needs of the students and to motivate students to participate directly in deciding what they will do to increase their learning. The role of the teacher becomes primarily that of planner, manager, and facilitator of learning activities. Also, the teacher is more free to respond to individual students. In church education there is increased emphasis on broadly graded and intergenerational classes. These approaches to teaching that lead to a more open classroom can increase the effectiveness of church teaching.

As a result of participating in this workshop persons will:

1. Hear and see an audio-visual presentation which introduces the concept of the open classroom and individualizing instruction.

2. Experience directly one or more learning centers or self-instructional modules.

3. Discuss the implications of individualizing instruction for teaching in the church.

4. Design one learning center activity or self-instructional module.

5. Preview a variety of resources available to guide teachers in planning for individualizing instruction.

BIBLIOGRAPHY

FOCUS ON KEY CONCEPTS

Elkind, David. A SYMPATHETIC UNDERSTANDING OF THE CHILD SIX TO SIXTEEN. Boston: Allyn & Bacon Inc., 1971.

Farth, Hans G. and Wachs, Harry. THINKING GOES TO SCHOOL: PIAGET'S THEORY IN PRACTICE. New York: Oxford University Press, 1974.

Godman, Ronald. RELIGIOUS THINKING FROM CHILDHOOD TO ADOLESCENCE. New York: Seabury Press, 1964.

Holt, John. HOW CHILDREN LEARN. New York: Pitman Publishing Corp., 1967.

FOCUS ON INSTRUCTIONAL OBJECTIVES

Kibler, Robert J., Barker, Larry L. and Miles, David T. BEHAVIORAL OBJECTIVES AND INSTRUCTION. Boston: Allyn and Bacon Inc., 1970.

Mager, Robert F. PREPARING INSTRUCTIONAL OBJECTIVES. Palo Alto: Fearson Publishers, 1962.

FOCUS ON TEACHING-LEARNING ACTIVITIES AND RESOURCES

Griggs, Donald L. TRANSLATING THE GOOD NEWS THROUGH TEACHING ACTIVITIES. Nashville: Abingdon, 1980.

Griggs, Patricia R. CREATIVE ACTIVITIES IN CHURCH EDUCATION, Nashville: Abingdon, 1980.

Leypoldt, Martha M. 40 WAYS TO TEACH IN GROUPS. Valley Forge: Judson Press, 1967.

Little, Sara. LEARNING TOGETHER IN THE CHRISTIAN FELLOWSHIP. Richmond: John Knox Press, 1966.

PRACTICE THE PLANNING PROCESS

Griggs, Donald L. THE PLANNING GAME. Nashville: Abingdon, 1980.

Washburn, John. TEACHING STRATEGY. Scottsdale, The Arizona Experiment, 1971.

INCREASING TEACHER-STUDENT INTERACTION

Bowman, Locke E. 70 CUES FOR TEACHERS. Scottsdale: The Arizona Experiment, 1972.

Bro, Marguerite Harmon. WHEN CHILDREN ASK. New York: Harper and Row, 1956.

Ginott, Haim G. TEACHER AND CHILD. New York: The MacMillan Co., 1972.

Hunter, Elizabeth. ENCOUNTER IN THE CLASSROOM. New York: Holt, Rinehart, and Winston, Inc., 1972.

Sanders, Norris M. CLASSROOM QUESTIONS, WHAT KIND? New York: Harper and Row, 1966.

CREATIVE USE OF MEDIA

McGuirk, Donn P. BETTER MEDIA FOR LESS MONEY! Scottsdale: The Arizona Experiment, 1972.

Morlan, John E. PREPARATION OF INEXPENSIVE TEACHING MATERIALS, 2nd Edition. New York: Chandler Publishing Co., 1973.

Ring, Arthur E. and Shelley, William J. LEARNING WITH THE OVERHEAD PROJECTOR. New York: Chandler Publishing Co., 1969.

VALUES AND TEACHING IN CHURCH EDUCATION

Raths, Louis E., Harmen, Merrill and Simon, Sidney B. VALUES AND TEACHING: WORKING WITH VALUES IN THE CLASSROOMS. Columbus: Charles E. Merrill Publishing Co., 1966.

Simon, Sidney B., Howe, Leland W., and Kirschenbaum, Howard. VALUES CLARIFICATION: A HANDBOOK OF PRACTICAL STRATEGIES FOR TEACHERS AND STUDENTS. New York: Hart Publishing Co., Inc., 1972.

WAYS TO INCREASE STUDENT PARTICIPATION

Barth, Roland S., OPEN EDUCATION AND THE AMERICAN SCHOOL. New York: Agathon Press Inc., 1972.

Morlan, John E. CLASSROOM LEARNING CENTERS. Belmont, California, Fearon Publishers, 1974.

DESIGNING TEACHER EDUCATION EVENTS

Bowman, Locke E. ESSENTIAL SKILLS FOR GOOD TEACHING, Scottsdale: The Arizona Experiment, 1974.

Bowman, Locke E. PLANNING FOR TEACHER EDUCATION IN THE PARISH. Philadelphia, Geneva Press, 1967.